PENGUIN BOOKS

cat vs. cat

Nationally renowned feline behaviorist Pam Johnson-Bennett is the author of five other award-winning books on cat behavior, including *Think Like a Cat: How to Raise a Well-Adjusted Cat Not a Sour Puss*, as well as an award-winning columnist. Pam is the resident cat expert at the popular Web site ivillage.com and was the behavior columnist for the Internet magazine *The Daily Cat* for a number of years. She has also written numerous behavioral articles for national magazines and was previously the behavior columnist for *Cats* magazine.

In addition to her busy private veterinarian-referred behavior practice, Pam is a popular guest on national TV and radio, and has spoken on the subject of behavior at veterinary conferences and animal welfare organizations.

Pam and her husband live in Tennessee with their daughter. They share their home with three cats, Albie, Mary Margaret, and Bebe. Albie had final approval on this book.

cat vs. cat

Keeping Peace When You Have More Than One Cat

PAM JOHNSON-BENNETT

FELINE BEHAVIORIST

penguin books

PENGUIN BOOKS

Published by the Penguin Group

Penguin Group (USA) Inc., 375 Hudson Street, New York, New York 10014, U.S.A.

Penguin Group (Canada), 90 Eglinton Avenue East, Suite 700, Toronto,
Ontario, Canada M4P 2Y3 (a division of Pearson Penguin Canada Inc.)

Penguin Books Ltd, 80 Strand, London WC2R 0RL, England

Penguin Ireland, 25 St Stephen's Green, Dublin 2, Ireland (a division of Penguin Books Ltd)

Penguin Group (Australia), 250 Camberwell Road, Camberwell,
Victoria 3124, Australia (a division of Pearson Australia Group Pty Ltd)

Penguin Books India Pvt Ltd, 11 Community Centre, Panchsheel Park, New Delhi – 110 017, India

Penguin Group (NZ), cnr Airborne and Rosedale Roads,
Albany, Auckland 1310, New Zealand (a division of Pearson New Zealand Ltd)

Penguin Books (South Africa) (Pty) Ltd, 24 Sturdee Avenue,
Rosebank, Johannesburg 2196, South Africa

Penguin Books Ltd, Registered Offices: 80 Strand, London WC2R 0RL, England

First published in Penguin Books 2004

10

LIBRARY OF CONGRESS CATALOGING-IN-PUBLICATION DATA
Johnson-Bennett, Pam, 1954–
Cat vs. cat : keeping peace when you have more than one cat /
Pam Johnson-Bennett.
p.   cm.
ISBN 0-14-200475-8
1. Cats—Behavior. 2. Cats—Psychology I. Title: Cat versus cat. II. Title.
SF446.5.J355 2004
636.8—dc22
2003067615

Printed in the United States of America
Set in Dante MT
Designed by Lynn Newmark

Scott, you make dreams come true.
This book is for you and Gracie,
and all of the cats waiting for their families at
the Rainbow Bridge.

ACKNOWLEDGMENTS

My biggest thank-you has to go to the cats who have trusted me and allowed me into their world all of these years. Every day they give me a renewed appreciation of their beauty, loyalty, grace, intelligence, and endless patience.

Thanks to Ellen Pryor; my agent, Linda Roghaar; my editor, Claire Hunsaker; and all of the wonderful people at Penguin Books. Steve Dale, thank you for being such a dear friend. The animals in our world are so lucky to have you watching out for them. Thanks to my home away from home—ivillage.com and the amazing people who help keep the message board and chat room running smoothly. My "CL's" on that board are the best, and I must give a special thanks to Barb.

CONTENTS

Introduction

Cats are the most popular pets in the United States, and so many of us share our lives with more than one. These beautiful creatures are clean, quiet, able to live indoors exclusively, and naturally take to eliminating in a litter box. It's so easy for many people to want to make the progression from one cat to two, three, or more.

However it has come to be, you are truly blessed to share your home and your heart with cats. There are so many joys in having more than one. Unfortunately, though, multicat families also face some unique problems. While *any* cat can experience a behavior problem, it certainly can become magnified in a multicat home. Heck, it can be harder just trying to figure out which cat is causing the problem.

I make many of my house calls to multicat homes, and the problem is often due to intercat relationship issues. Maybe the owner didn't know how to properly introduce the cats, or maybe the cats are jockeying for a better position in the hierarchy, or maybe territorial disagreements have led to a litter box problem. All too often, owners don't know enough about *how* cats live together, so they don't understand how to create an environment that inspires peaceful coexistence. We love cats so much, but we don't realize that they are essentially territorial. When we ask them to live close together, they have less personal space, and a smaller territory causes them a lot of stress. Overcrowding can create tremendous anxiety and turn a happy home into a war zone. Cats give us so much and we have a responsibility to create an environment in which everyone can feel happy, safe, and secure.

This book will teach you how to avoid multicat household behavior problems and will also help if you're in the middle of a crisis right now. I've written this to be a companion to my book on general cat care and training, *Think Like a Cat*. If you're a first-time cat parent or considering becoming one, I recommend that you read *Think Like a Cat* to get a good foundation in the basics of care and training. *Cat Vs. Cat* will then provide you with valuable insight into how cats communicate both with humans and other cats. When you learn the "whys" behind behavior, you'll better understand what cats need from you, their environment, and each other. That way, if you decide to join the family of multicat parents, you'll be able to avoid many behavior problems and simply enjoy those fuzzy bundles of love.

If you're a seasoned cat parent, this book will help you sharpen your detective skills and solve current problems. You'll be able to take a step back to observe your multicat environment in a more objective way, figure out the causes, and then map out a behavior modification plan. Whether your situation just needs a little tweaking or a major overhaul, you'll find techniques in this book to get you and your cats back on track.

I'd also like to address one issue right up front because the rest of this book is absolutely secondary to this: *You must spay and neuter your cats.* Intact cats cannot coexist peacefully. Intact males will definitely spray and fight. If allowed outdoors, intact males will roam, fight, and indiscriminately mate. Unspayed females will "call" repeatedly, attract unwanted cats into your yard, and constantly try to escape out the door. Intact animals are also at a higher risk of developing certain types of cancers. Cats who are not spayed or neutered are ruled by their hormones. They don't make good pets by themselves and are impossible to maintain in a multicat home.

I am the parent of three cats. Albie I adopted as a very young kitten and Mary Margaret and Bebe came into my life as ferals. Bebe needs a great deal of personal space in order to feel secure. I've set up my home to allow for that so she has special places she can go when she needs "alone time." All of my cats are spayed and neutered and live exclusively indoors. By better understanding what they need and how to create a secure and enriching environment, we all live together in peace. When I come home and find a couple of the kitties curled up together, it just melts my heart. My wish is that you are able to enjoy many of those heart-melting moments as well.

cat

vs.

cat

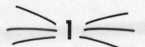

Understanding the Feline Hierarchy

You may look at your multicat household as one happy family; you love your cats equally and feel there shouldn't be any reason for fighting or squabbling. In reality, though, your cats don't view *each other* as equals, nor should they. Whether you have two cats or twenty, there is a pecking order. It may bother you to think that a few cats reign supreme over others, but hierarchy is necessary in feline society. In a free-roaming situation, it prevents overcrowding of the colony and gives cats a sense of order and security.

CATS ARE SOCIAL CREATURES

Many people believe cats to be solitary creatures. That mistaken belief in part stems from the fact that cats hunt alone. As a small animal, a cat hunts small prey, which isn't much of a motivator for cooperation. This makes the cat look all the more like a loner.

Another behavior that adds to the cat's mistakenly labeled reputation as asocial is his territorial instinct. One example of how we recognize dogs as social creatures is because existing canine households will often easily accept a new puppy. When cat owners think of adding another kitty, visions of hissing, scratching, fights, and, in general, disaster, come to mind. This hardly inspires one to label a cat as *social*. But being territorial doesn't exclude a cat from being social. It's just important to work out territorial issues before two cats can become friends and have fun.

The social communities in the feline world vary, from very independent ferals who hunt and live alone to domesticated indoor cats who share very close quarters. In the case of indoor cats, the owner is the primary food source, except perhaps for the occasional unlucky mouse who finds himself cornered in the kitchen late at night.

In an outdoor environment, a cat's socialness will depend mostly on the availability of food and shelter. Cats will coexist in closer proximity to each other near a common food source or shelter. Even in those situations, most of the cats may avoid each other and "live alone" in a group. Between the independent ferals and the dependent indoor cats you'll find free-roaming cats: ferals who interact minimally, and owned cats who have access to the outdoors.

The most common social relationship is between a female cat and her kittens. With indoor cats, kittens are generally separated

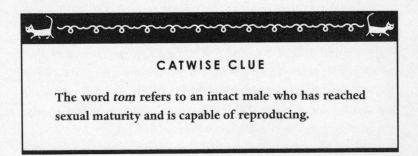

CATWISE CLUE

The word *tom* refers to an intact male who has reached sexual maturity and is capable of reproducing.

from the mother too early for a happy, healthy adoption. (Kittens *should* be kept with the mother and littermates for twelve weeks.) In free-roaming environments, kittens usually stay with the mother longer. Female kittens, once they leave the mother, will generally stay within the same area, whereas males will travel farther.

Some females in a colony may form communal nests and nurse one another's kittens. This benefits the mothers who are not as strong, so all of the kittens have a better chance at survival. Females commonly move their kittens often if they fear attacks from males or outside predators. In free-roaming cats, long-term bonds aren't formed between mating partners. There's nothing romantic about sex in the feline world. It's all about survival.

In multicat homes the cats may only tolerate one another, or some cats in the hierarchy may form very close bonds. Much of this will depend on how well the cats were socialized, how they were introduced, their personalities, their understanding of the territorial divisions, and how the owner has handled potential squabbling.

STATUS

Although there is a general hierarchy in your cat household, it's not a pecking order forever set in stone. The hierarchy is dynamic and subtly shifts and moves. When a hierarchy is well established, the security and familiarity of knowing where they stand allows the cats to coexist peacefully. But in some households the delicate hierarchy remains in balance only by a whisker. One or two cats may "rule the roost," or subtle shifts in status can occur depending on who is in the room and what events are taking place. One cat may claim the owner's bedroom and another cat may be more dominant at the feeding station.

I think of the feline hierarchy as the rungs of a ladder. The highest-ranking cat sits on top. In a perfect world, each new cat added to the household would take his place at the next highest available rung. Oh, if only it could be that simple, there wouldn't be so many squabbles. Unfortunately, though, a new cat may be more assertive and might attempt to knock another cat off an attractive rung. As you can well imagine, that never sits well with the existing cat community, and, all of a sudden, the rungs on the ladder get a bit shaky. If you're going from one cat to two, your resident cat may willingly step down from his top rung (it's easy to be top cat when there are no other cats in the house). He may feel more comfortable taking a lower status if the new cat is more confident.

The rungs of an actual ladder are evenly spaced, but the rungs on a feline hierarchy ladder aren't. Some cats may be relatively close in status, so their rungs may just be a whisker's width apart. Other cats may be separated by very wide gaps. This unevenness in the spaces is one reason why the hierarchy may hit bumps in the road. The competition between two cats close in rank may routinely ignite the anxiety of one, and they will be more likely to engage in physical confrontation. A middle-ranking cat may repeatedly pick on a very low-ranking cat, especially if he has been the target of the cats above him. Since he doesn't feel confident enough to stand up to the more senior cats, he turns his frustrations on a cat beneath him.

Observation of the actual vertical territory within your home can provide clues about the pecking order. Height plays a crucial role in the hierarchy. The cat who is able to access and control the highest elevations in the environment will likely develop the higher status. It provides the cat with the ability to oversee his domain, and demonstrates his dominance to subordinates. But it also might help reduce conflict because the cat may choose to go to his perch to show indifference and dominance rather than engage in active aggression.

The physical position of the cats as they enter a room can also provide clues as to who is in charge in that area or at that particular time. For example: two cats enter the room and one walks toward the middle of the space while the other walks along the perimeter. The one occupying the center of the room may give a direct stare to the perimeter cat. The perimeter cat avoids direct eye contact. The center cat has control of the room.

In a tense environment, cats who are less prone to anxiety tend to be higher ranking. This stands to reason because when the group faces a stressful situation, it needs leaders who are calmer and more able to think clearly. The dominant cat in the household may not be the one who demonstrates the most aggressive behavior, but actually the calmest cat of the bunch.

Cats close in status are more likely to engage in an actual physical confrontation. These cats may be on the "middle" rungs of the hierarchy ladder. A clearly higher-ranking cat may act nonchalant and walk away from a tense situation or groom himself. Acting indifferent can appear more intimidating. It works to his advantage not to display weakness.

Higher-ranking cats may posture instead of entering into actual aggressive confrontations. Posturing is an important precursor to any potentially aggressive encounter. Guarding choice areas is a common example: a higher-ranking cat may block the pathway to the litter box or food bowl, or might stay in the litter box longer and be the first one to use it after it has been cleaned.

Higher-ranking cats frequently claim the prime areas of a territory. For some cats that may be the owner's bed. For others, it could be the soft chair by the fireplace or the window that overlooks the outdoor bird feeder.

Sometimes a higher-ranking cat may entice a lower-ranking one into his territory and then attack him for trespassing.

Sometimes when a number of cats share a territory, you'll find one who is the *pariah*. This is the lowest-ranking cat, and he will stay far away from the others. The pariah lives on the perimeter of the territory, walks low to the ground, and will usually growl when in the vicinity of another cat. You may find him slinking to the food station to grab leftovers long after the other cats have eaten.

Mounting behavior in altered cats, whether between males or females, is often a dominance display. This may surprise and alarm owners, but it's important to realize that it isn't a sexual display. In some cat colonies, low-ranking males may submit to being mounted by cats of higher status. Or cats may masturbate in a colony where there is ongoing tension. This may be a way for an anxious cat to self-soothe. Don't worry, it doesn't mean your cat was incorrectly neutered.

How a cat interacts with you doesn't influence his rank in the hierarchy. A dominant cat, however, may display the same status-related behavior toward a human as he would another cat—such as direct staring, rubbing and then backing away as a challenge, mouthing.

What determines a cat's place in the hierarchy? There are many factors such as age, size, sexual maturity, social maturity, number of cats in the colony, whether the cat had littermates and how they interacted, health, the availability of food, the list goes on. That's not to say that the biggest cat will automatically be the most dominant, but if you're a big strapping tom, you sure have the advantage when it comes to physical posturing.

EARLY SOCIALIZATION

If you are breeding your cat or have found yourself with a pregnant female, socializing the young kittens is very important. It can make a big difference in how they respond to humans as they mature. Frequent, gentle handling by more than one person can help the kittens become less-fearful adults. Kittens should be handled frequently and very gently, starting at two weeks of age.

The critical socialization period is between two and seven weeks, but actually, it's still beneficial as late as nine weeks.

During these first two weeks, the kittens need to nurse, sleep, and stay warm by being snuggled close to mom.

This is an important time for mother and kittens to bond and establish a routine. If you interfere prior to two weeks, the mother might become agitated and move her nest. For the mother, this early time is crucial for her to feel secure and calm about the safety of her nest.

Kittens should ideally stay with the mother and littermates for twelve weeks. Kittens that are weaned and able to successfully eliminate in the litter box may appear ready for adoption as early as six to eight weeks, but there are many psychological advantages to keeping them in the nest until they're twelve weeks old. Kittens taken away from the nest too early or raised without littermates don't learn some very important social skills. They may overreact (that is, bite too hard) during play or social interactions. That extra time in the nest helps the kittens accept other cats in the environment more easily and interact more appropriately with them. In some cases, they may still only reach a level of tolerance, but they could also form strong social attachments.

Littermates engage in social play with each other at around three weeks of age, as the kittens are able to move around more easily. Each week you'll notice the social play get more refined as the kittens become more adept at balance and coordination. As the kittens get older, they engage in less social play and in more object play. By twelve weeks of age, their play patterns may begin to resemble fighting more than playing. You may start to notice more hissing, crying during wrestling, and more serious posturing.

BUMPS IN THE ROAD

There are some situations that cause rumblings throughout the hierarchy in your cat household. The addition or subtraction of a cat, a new home, illness or death in the feline colony, and sexual maturity are the types of upheavals most likely to affect cats. There are also some not-so-obvious reasons for a sudden shakeup. One event many owners aren't aware of is *social maturity*. This occurs between two and four years of age and is not to be confused with *sexual maturity*, which occurs around six to seven months. Almost all owners are aware of the fact that a kitten officially becomes an adult at the age of one year, but the cat still has more maturing to do in the social department. Much like human adolescence, social maturity is the prime time for cats to jockey for social positions. This may cause subtle and not-so-subtle shifting in the pecking order in a formerly peaceful, well-established cat family. This can be a time when a cat feels more confident and views an opportunity to elevate his status.

Illness also plays a role in the hierarchy that you may not be prepared for. An ill cat loses his current position and usually becomes subordinate to all of the other healthy ones, regardless of previous status.

CAN YOU HAVE TOO MANY CATS?

There is a situation where a "bump in the road" turns into a brick wall, and that is when you simply have too many cats. Because of space considerations and the different personalities of each individual cat, it's important to recognize a healthy limit to the size of your family. Although cats require less space than dogs, there is only so much physical territory to go around. You won't be doing your cats a favor if they're forced to live in uncomfortably close quarters in a constantly hostile environment. Don't turn into a cat hoarder. The quality of your cats' lives, as well as your own, will suffer.

Many factors must also be taken into consideration when determining how many cats can live together under one roof. Your next-door neighbor may have five cats who coexist peacefully, while your three can't seem to come to a truce even though your home and your neighbor's are exactly the same. How the cats were socialized, how they were introduced, the number of dominant cats, and the specific dynamics of your household all play a role in how well the cats live together. You may have one cat who simply should've been an only cat. There are some cats, just as there are some people, who are happiest not having to share space.

You also have to consider the cost of keeping multiple cats. In addition to the cost of food, there are ongoing veterinary expenses. Your responsibility as a cat owner doesn't end with saving a cat from the side of the road—you are also responsible for making sure the cat's medical needs are met. While many owners are lucky enough only to have the yearly expenses of routine vaccinations and checkups, others aren't so fortunate and may end up with one or more cats who require special food, prescriptions, ongoing monitoring, or even extensive diagnostic tests or surgery. Veterinary medicine has grown by leaps and bounds, and it's amazing what can be done to keep our precious cats living longer. But those advancements come with a price.

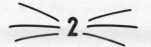

The Complex World
of Feline Communication

Cats are true masters at communication. While we humans rely on verbal communicating, cats use three forms: *scent, body language,* and *vocalization.*

For territorial animals who choose to avoid conflict whenever possible, maximizing communication skills can mean the difference between injury and safety and, in some cases, life and death. The more skilled you are at being able to interpret what your cats are communicating, the better able you'll be at heading off potential intercat feuds. You'll be able, we hope, to determine who is being offensive and who is being defensive. Even when it comes to an individual kitty, the more you know about what she's communicating, the better off you'll both be. If you are an owner who gets scratched or bitten quite often, you may be misreading your kitty's cues. Be a little more informed, and you might end up with fewer scars.

CATWISE REMINDER

It can be very confusing to try to interpret what a cat is feeling and communicating if you look only at one aspect. You have to take everything into consideration—eyes, ears, whiskers, body posture, vocalization (if any), and environmental circumstances.

EYES*

* *Round pupils*—interest, excitement, fear, or defensive aggression.

* *Constricted pupils*—offensive aggression.

* *Slightly oval pupils*—relaxation.

* *Unblinking stare*—dominance or defensive threat.

* *Relaxed, almost droopy lids*—trust and relaxation.

EARS

* *Held erect and forward facing*—alert, interested.

* *Turned sideways, a.k.a. "airplane wings"*—concern or fear about a possible threat. This ear position can also indicate ear discomfort or an ear infection.

---

*It's important to note that pupil size also varies with light and can also indicate an injury or medical condition.

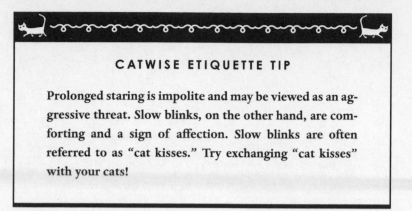

CATWISE ETIQUETTE TIP

Prolonged staring is impolite and may be viewed as an aggressive threat. Slow blinks, on the other hand, are comforting and a sign of affection. Slow blinks are often referred to as "cat kisses." Try exchanging "cat kisses" with your cats!

* *Rotated to the side and downward*—defensive aggression.

* *Rotated back and completely flattened*—extreme defensive aggression.

* *Rotated back and flattened, but with some of the inner ear flaps* (pinnae) *visible*—extreme offensive aggression.

TAIL

* *Vertical, erect, and slightly curled*—friendliness. Cat is most likely looking to interact.

* *Piloerection (hairs on end)*—increased anxiety that may be due to either defensive or passive aggressive state.

* *Wrapped around body*—distance-increasing posture that says the cat is either fearful or not wanting to interact.

* *Inverted "U"*—defensive aggression (young kittens may assume this tail position during play).

* *Arched and positioned over the back*—usually a defensive display. If the opponent doesn't back down, the cat may lower its tail—without piloerection it can also indicate interest or arousal.

* *Mild flicking*—irritation.

* *Thumping*—conflict, frustration, irritation.

* *Lashing*—agitation. The greater the lashing, the greater the agitation. The cat is giving you a very clear warning to "back off."

WHISKERS

* *Rotated forward*—interest or aggression, depending on circumstances, ear position, and body posture. If the ears are rotated sideways or back, then the cat is communicating aggression. If the ears are in a normal alert position (pricked forward), then the cat's interest may have been sparked as in the case of spotting prey.

* *Relaxed slightly, pointed sideways (not forward or back)*—normal relaxed position.

* *Flattened back along cheeks*—fear. The cat is hoping to appear as small as possible.

HAIR

* *Piloerection*—defensive state.

* *Standing up a little but not full-fledged piloerection*—a sense of unease, but also not threatened enough to feel escape is necessary.

* *Lowered*—offensive aggression (if tail is stiffly moving) or defensive aggression (if movements aren't as stiff).

* *Horizontal (half lowered)*—relaxed. This is the normal tail position.

* *Between legs*—submission.

VOCALIZATION

Purr—A vibrating motorlike sound produced during times of contentment and also anxiety. In anxious situations it may serve to self-soothe and also to calm an opponent. A nursing mother purrs so her kittens can locate her by feeling the vibrations. Cats may also purr when very sick or injured, possibly to self-soothe.

Meow—A greeting usually reserved for humans.

Mew—A sound used for identification and location purposes between cats.

Grunt—Vocalization of newborn kittens.

Moan—A mournful, lonely, and long sound that some cats make before vomiting or hairball regurgitation. Some older cats may moan during the night if they become disoriented or confused by the sudden quiet of the household. Some cats also moan when sitting at the front door begging to be let out or in.

Chirp—A sound given by a cat when she sees something desirable that she's about to receive. Usually a meal or a treat, but can also be a wanted interaction with an owner. Mothers may also use this sound with their kittens.

Trill—A sound similar to a chirp but a little more musical in sound. It's a happy sound.

Growl—This is a low-pitched sound produced with an open mouth that can be offensive or defensive. It's one of the cat's verbal warning sounds.

Hiss—A snakelike sound produced with an open mouth that is usually defensive. The cat arches her tongue and quickly forces air out of her mouth to make the sound. If you're directly in front of the cat you can actually feel the force of air.

Spit—A sudden, short, airy, poppinglike sound that usually follows or precedes a hiss.

CATWISE ETIQUETTE TIP

The proper way to pick up a cat is to place one hand beneath the cat's bottom in order to support the weight and prevent the hind legs from dangling. Place your other hand under the cat's chest so she can rest her front paws on your arm. Hold her close to your body, but don't make her feel confined.

Murmur—A soft sound made with a closed mouth that usually accompanies purring or is given as a greeting.

Squeak—A raspy, high-pitched sound usually done when the cat anticipates meal preparation. Also done during play.

Shriek—A harsh, high-pitched sound given out when in pain or during extreme aggressive encounters.

Chattering—A sound indicating excitement at the sight of prey, usually done when the cat can't physically get to the prey (seeing a bird through the window, for example).

Snarl—An intimidating expression where the upper lip curls, exposing the teeth. This may or may not be accompanied by a growl.

POSTURE

Body posture can be classified into two categories: *distance increasing* and *distance reducing*. Basically, a cat's body posture is saying, "Go away" or "It's okay to come closer." Interestingly, the posture can quickly change based on the cat's comfort level. It might start out saying, "It's okay to come closer" but may switch to "That's far enough" or even "I've changed my mind . . . go away!"

A cat in an offensive, aggressive state walks on tiptoe with a lowered head. Whiskers forward, ears erect but rotated sideways, claws visible, pupils constricted. Subordinate cats may crouch or flee the immediate area. If a rival cat approaches, the two may try to stare each other down like slow-motion gunslingers. They may walk slightly past each other and then the aggressor may pounce. The defensive cat may immediately roll over into the belly-up position to engage all weapons. A confident, dominant cat approaches head-on with a direct gaze. A shy, fearful, or subordinate cat presents a profile and avoids direct stares. The cat who just calmly walked away and turned her back was the victor in a subtle standoff.

Below are descriptions of some body postures to help you better interpret what your cats may be trying to communicate:

Crouching—defensiveness. The tail will usually be tucked closely around the body. This protects the tail and makes the cat appear smaller and less threatening to an opponent. A fearful cat will press its ears back and down. An extremely fearful cat will usually drool.

Legs held straight with hindquarters slightly elevated—offensiveness. The cat's hind legs are longer than the front, so this stiff-legged posture is easy.

Belly Up—This ultimate defensive posture allows the cat to engage her teeth and all four sets of claws. This posture is also a warning that lets the opponent know that should he agree to back down, no interaction will take place. On the other hand, a sleeping or relaxed cat may also stretch out on her back, exposing her belly, where she is most vulnerable. This is a sign of total relaxation but may trigger a defensive reaction if you pet the cat's stomach or if another cat approaches. The degree of the defensive reaction depends on the individual cat.

Kittens may display the belly-up position as a demonstration of play. You have to observe accompanying signals to be sure. If the kitten's ears are forward, then she's in a play mode. If the ears are rotated back, then her belly-up posi-

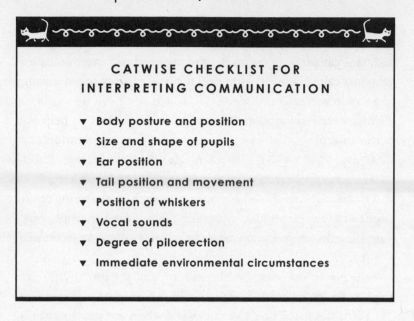

CATWISE CHECKLIST FOR INTERPRETING COMMUNICATION

▼ Body posture and position

▼ Size and shape of pupils

▼ Ear position

▼ Tail position and movement

▼ Position of whiskers

▼ Vocal sounds

▼ Degree of piloerection

▼ Immediate environmental circumstances

tion is defensive. If the kitten is soliciting play, then she'll probably meow or trill, but if she's defending herself, she'll hiss.

Side-to-side rolling—play solicitation, greeting.

Arched back with piloerection of hair—This "Halloween cat" posture can be an offensive or defensive display. It communicates that the cat is ready to do whatever is necessary in reaction to the opponent's next move. From the arched back position the cat may switch to offensive or defensive aggression. It's the cat's way of warning the opponent to think twice about his next move.

Kittens may display this posture during social play. They may go up on tiptoe and do a comical crablike walk while soliciting another kitten to play.

SCENT COMMUNICATION

Marking behavior is the cat's primary form of communication, and boy are they ever equipped for it! Cats can mark through urine, feces, claws, and scent glands. Marking can be visual, olfactory, or a combination of both.

SPECIAL EQUIPMENT Cats come equipped with a very special "scent analyzer" called a *vomeronasal organ* or *Jacobson's organ,* located above the roof of the mouth. It's used for analyzing pheromones (scent chemicals), especially those found in urine, but a cat will enlist its help whenever she comes across an interesting scent.

The scent is collected in the mouth, and the tongue transfers it up to the ducts located just behind the front teeth. These ducts lead into the nasal cavity. You can tell when the cat is engaging the Jacobson's organ because her mouth will be partially open with the upper lip curled. The expression, which resembles a grimace, is known as the *flehman* response.

Although all cats are equipped with the specialized scent organ, it's used most often by intact males when they come across the urine of a female in heat.

URINE-MARKING If you haven't had to deal with a cat who urine-marks, you are very lucky. The higher the cat density in your home, the greater the chances that you will have to deal with this behavior. Spraying is a very effective form of communication, and cats use it to mark territory, threaten, announce their arrival, engage in dispute without confronting each other, or exchange information.

This is an unpleasant dialogue for people to be caught in, but you can prevent a urine-marking situation from ever developing.

The behavior modification techniques to help if you're in the middle of this crisis right now are covered in chapter 7.

RUBBING Rubbing is an intricate and important factor in the social lives of cats. Cats are covered in sebaceous glands that release pheromones, which contain information about the particular cat. By smelling this information, either on the cat or on something rubbed, other cats can tell whether it's a male or female, sexually available, and how long ago the scent was left. The glands are concentrated on the lips, forehead, chin, tail, and paw pads, but cats may also rub objects with their flanks to leave scent deposits. Cats might rub inanimate objects, other cats, humans, and companion dogs. For inanimate objects they tend to use their cheeks, and when rubbing another animal, they might combine this with head, flank, and tail rubbing.

Rubbing inanimate objects is one way a cat marks territory and leaves information about herself for other cats. If the targeted object is high, the cat may rub the underside using her forehead. Very low objects may be rubbed with the underside of the chin. In some households with multiple males, you may notice that the higher-ranking ones tend to do more facial rubbing on objects than the lower-ranking ones.

Rubbing isn't exclusively used for scent release. It's also one way a cat collects or combines scents—especially when flank rubbing. This can be a social behavior used for bonding and also a show of respect from a lower-ranking cat to a higher-ranking one.

When a cat rubs her head on an owner or another animal, she is depositing pheromones and it's referred to as *bunting*. Bunting is often a bonding behavior and may also be related to status, depending on the circumstances.

When you come home from work at the end of the day and

your cats engage in cheek rubbing, flank rubbing, and bunting, it is their way of giving you the familiar colony scent again.

Before rubbing, a cat usually raises her tail as she approaches. If there's another familiar cat approaching her and she also raises her tail, it's possibly a signal that both cats intend to engage in *allorubbing*.

Cats most often use their incredibly keen sense of smell to recognize one another. Cats living together may rub one another to create a familiar colony scent. This is a survival instinct because it helps to more quickly identify whether a cat entering the territory is familiar or an intruder. Allogrooming (mutual grooming) is part of the social structure. It's generally restricted to cats who are friendly and who will normally share napping and resting areas.

One cat may lick the head of another cat as an invitation to play. Either this is welcome and results in a game of chase and play wrestling, or it's ill timed and results in a swat to the nose of the initiator.

When two familiar cats approach each other in a nonhostile situation, they will start with nose-to-nose sniffing, head rubbing, and possibly licking the face and ears. Anal sniffing is next. The cat who elicits the first rub is usually more dominant. If the cats are not friendly, then the exchange will end at nose sniffing.

When your cat jumps in your lap, goes nose to nose with you, and then turns to present her backside, you may have considered this unpleasant, but it's actually very polite in terms of feline social etiquette. Another often misinterpreted behavior is when a cat lounges with her back toward you. What she's really saying in both situations is that she trusts you.

When a cat exhibits head-rubbing behavior to an unfamiliar human (such as a guest in your home) immediately upon meeting and then steps back and stares, it's often a hierarchical challenge. Humans often misinterpret this behavior as friendly and then end up getting scratched or bitten when they reach down to stroke the cat.

When greeting an unfamiliar cat, extend your index finger and let her approach for a sniff. This is similar to nose-to-nose sniffing that cats do. Don't reach to pet the cat, just leave your finger extended. After the cat does a scent investigation, she may then rub the side of her mouth along your finger or even rub her head or side of her body. This is her way of letting you know that she's at ease with you. At that point, you can offer to pet her. Don't pet her until she has finished her scent investigation, and don't pet her if she backs up and stares at you.

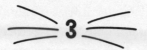

The Importance of Territory

TURF 101

In a free-roaming environment, a cat's area is divided up into different sections. These divisions are clearly defined from a cat's point of view. The outermost area where the cat roams and patrols for food is referred to as the *home range,* and may overlap other cats' areas as well. Adult males tend to have a larger home range than females, and during mating season, an intact male's home range will increase temporarily as he seeks to mate. In the home range, a cat is more likely to flee than engage in conflict.

Inward from the home range is the cat's actual *territory.* This is the area a cat will defend against intruders. If an intruder enters, the cat who owns the territory has the psychological "home field" advantage. A cat's home range and territory are two separate areas. For indoor cats, the home range and territory are obviously smaller, and they overlap or are combined into one due to the physical limitations of the four walls. A cat may permit another familiar social companion cat to enter his territory up to a certain point.

The innermost part of the territory is the cat's *personal space.* He may allow a social companion into this space or the cat may be driven back to a more acceptable distance. As with people, every cat is an individual, some need very small personal spaces, and others need a more extensive zone around them.

Indoor cats divide up territories within the home just as free-roaming cats do outdoors. Because there's a plentiful food source, though, they don't have to compete for food, so most of the time there is less stress on territory definitions.

TIME-SHARES

No, I'm not talking about the condo in Miami that your aunt bought. I'm referring to territory time-sharing. Cats are experts at developing time-share schedules, and this is a major part of how multiple cats can share a limited space. One cat may occupy a certain room or sleep on a piece of furniture at a particular time of day, and then another cat claims it during the next shift. This isn't just a coincidence, but rather a delicate balance of peace through avoidance. Trouble occurs when one cat chooses to occupy an area at the off schedule. A wise kitty defers to the cat who normally resides there at that time, but every now and then a cat doesn't play by the rules. Not all objects will be open for time-share negotiations. Certain favorite spots, while not occupied by the particular cat twenty-four hours a day, are not used by the other cats, either.

When you stop to think about how carefully the cats have worked out the time-sharing arrangement, you can begin to appreciate how upsetting it must be when furniture is rearranged, certain pieces are removed, a new cat is added, or you make a move to a new home.

MOVIN' ON UP

If you're thinking like a human, you view your home as one territory. Whether it has one room or one hundred rooms, it's still basically *your* territory. However, if you're thinking like a cat, you can see your home as numerous territories on many different levels, levels that are an important part of maintaining the hierarchy.

Here's a way to visualize the importance of levels. Imagine the living room in your home without any furniture—just the carpet, walls, and windows. If you put your cats in there, they would probably head for opposite corners because there's only one level. The higher-ranking cats wouldn't have areas of elevation, and everyone would be stressed and unsure about where they were supposed to be. Now, imagine putting one chair in there. Immediately, one kitty would probably rub on it and hop up (probably a higher-ranking cat). Another kitty would very likely hide beneath the chair. If it's a big, upholstered armchair, you might even find that one cat perches on the high back and one or two occupy the arms and one sits on the seat itself. Just by adding one chair you increased the territory using multiple levels. Now, imagine adding a table, another chair, a bookcase, a cat tree, and so forth. With every piece of furniture, you add more territory. What was once a one-level, open, vulnerable area is now a more secure, comfortable environment where cats can better maintain their personal spaces and time-share.

Look around your entire home with all the furniture in it. You probably see the more dominant cats in the highest areas and the timid or low-ranking cats in more hidden or secure areas. There's probably a cat on the refrigerator (or at least a determined one trying to get up there) because that's usually the highest perch in the home. There may be a cat who finds a way to do a daring leap from the bed to the top of the armoire in the master bedroom. In that same bedroom there might also be a cat hidden under the bed behind the shoe boxes or plastic sweater containers stored there. Cats make use of every available inch of vertical space and all the various levels in their environment.

If you don't allow your cats on any of the furniture, this may be one reason why there's tension between the cats; they aren't able to establish areas relative to their hierarchy.

HOW TO INCREASE TERRITORY

If you've ever been to a cat sanctuary or even seen pictures of one, you may have marveled at how so many cats could live together. If you look closely, though, you'd see all the various levels. There are shelves, perches, and cat trees at varying heights—many extending up to the ceiling.

As you look around your home, there is probably a great deal of unused vertical space that could be converted into areas for cat access. Now, if you were an owner of a single cat, just your furniture would probably be sufficient to provide adequate levels, along with a nice cat tree. As a multicat owner, however, adequate territorial space is more of an issue; unless you plan on breaking down a wall and building on to your home, your best option is to build *up*.

When it comes to increasing vertical territory, you can get as elaborate or basic as you'd like, depending on your taste and budget. From a cat's point of view, vertical areas just need to be:

* Safe

* Comfortable

* Easy to ascend and descend

* Well located

CAT TREES One of the quickest and easiest ways to increase territory is by adding multiperched cat trees. If you get a tree with two or more perches, a couple of cats can share a relatively close space and still maintain a comfortable distance. Two cats who normally wouldn't sit side by side on a windowsill to watch the birds may peacefully share the tree because of the different levels of perches.

A cat tree is also a great way to help a timid cat choose to stay in a room when company visits. When I took in my formerly feral cat, Bebe, all she wanted to do was hide. We had created a sanctuary room for her in our sunroom, but she dove behind the couch whenever I entered. When I wasn't in the room, however, she loved being in her cat tree. To help her feel more hidden and secure, I bought some silk tree branches from my local craft store and wired them to the cat tree, and I strategically placed some silk trees in front of her cat tree and around the room. (I used silk trees instead of live plants because it would be safer for the cat.) The branches disguised the perches, and Bebe felt securely hidden enough to remain in the tree whenever I entered. With the trees placed around the room, she also started feeling secure enough to venture around (when no one was in the room) onto furniture so she could look out of other windows.

Bebe would watch me from her tree as I sat on the carpet casually dragging a fishing pole toy along the ground. I'd see her beautiful eyes peering at me from between the silk leaves. After a few sessions of enticement, I noticed her eyes were no longer focused on me as much as they were on the toy. Slowly but surely, Bebe inched her way down the tree, perch by perch, and eventually pounced on the toy. She was beginning to trust me, because being in the cat tree had enabled her to observe me from a safe distance. If she had just stayed behind the couch, it might have taken much longer for her to feel secure enough to peek around the corner at me.

You can buy cat trees at just about any pet supply store. They are also available through mail-order companies and on the Internet. There are some companies that will custom design a tree for you based on your specifications for height, number, and style of perches, and even type/color of carpet. Take a quick search on the Internet, and you'll find several cat tree manufacturers. If there's a cat show coming to your area, that's a great place to see cat trees up close and personal. There are usually several cat tree vendors at the shows, and you can buy a tree right there or order one to be delivered later. You can also check the ads in the back of cat-related magazines for cat tree manufacturers. If ordering a tree you haven't actually seen, ask the manufacturer about how the tree is made, how sturdy it is, how heavy the base is, the return policy, and so forth. Not all trees are created equal.

When shopping for trees, make sure the perches are wide and comfortable. Some trees have square, flat perches, and others have curved U-shaped ones. I find the cats tend to prefer the curved ones, which may give a cat an added feeling of security and prevent her from rolling off the perch while asleep. The U-shaped perches also provide a bit more cover for a cat so he can duck down and peer over the side if watching a bird at the window, or if he just needs that extra bit of concealment for emotional security.

Cat trees also do double duty as scratching posts. You can find trees with support posts wrapped in sisal, the scratching texture favored by many cats. You can also find trees covered with bare wood or bark, and some of the larger trees with more support posts can have various coverings so you can satisfy the sisal scratcher as well as the bare-wood scratcher in your home.

Trees come as freestanding or mountable to the ceiling (usually tension-mounted). The freestanding trees tend to have wider, more comfortable perches and are easier to relocate. I think the freestanding may be more secure than the tension-mounted as long as you get a sturdy one with a wide, heavy base. The taller the tree, the heavier and wider the base should be. If the tree you're shopping for seems the least bit top-heavy, don't even consider buying it because one good leap from a cat could topple the thing over. Even if the tree doesn't actually fall over but only wobbles, that instability can deter cats from returning to it.

If you're a do-it-yourselfer, you may want to make a tree. Before you do, though, check out the trees at pet supply stores and those online so you'll have a good idea of how to shape and size the perches. My father made a cat tree out of some thick branches from a tree that fell in his yard after a storm. The cat tree didn't cost much to construct, and it became a conversation piece. When company visited, the cats loved to show off their tree and would lounge on it in the most charming positions.

In terms of placement, you may be tempted to stick cat trees in empty, unused corners, but your cats will enjoy and use them much more if they're by windows, especially sunny ones for those lazy afternoon naps and optimal bird-watching. If you're bringing in several trees, place them in the rooms where the cats spend the most time, but don't overlook opportunities for behavior modification. An example: If you have a couple of cats who compete for space on your bed at night, think about putting a tree in the bedroom. You may be able to entice one of the cats to sleep there at night. Some owners place the tree in out-of-the-way locations because they don't care for the look of them. Most of your cats will want to be where you are, so don't hide the trees in unused rooms unless you're placing them there for a specific kitty who has camped out.

When you first bring a cat tree into the house, you can rub some catnip on the support posts as a nice introduction for your cats. If your cats get upset by new furniture, lay a T-shirt or towel that contains your scent over each perch for a few days. Unless you are trying to provide a tree for a specific cat, it's best to use an article that has *your* scent as opposed to your cats' scents because you don't know who is going to claim the tree. This way, they can work it out for themselves. You can also spray Feliway on the perches (see chapter 7 for more on this product).

When you first start shopping for cat trees, you may get hit with sticker shock. Don't despair because there's a wide range of prices, depending upon how elaborate you want to get. It'll be a complete waste of money to buy an inexpensive tree if the cats won't use it because the perches are too small or the tree isn't sta-ble. On the other hand, if budget is a concern, choose a simple, sturdy tree without the fancy extras (preinstalled toys, color-coordinated carpet, and so forth). Even though a strong, sturdy tree may be more expensive than you were anticipating, a well-made one will last for many years. The first tree I bought twenty years ago is still going strong. Angelical Cat Company makes sev-eral types of sturdy trees. You can find the company's informa-tion in the Appendix.

You may be tempted, especially if you have kittens in your home, to buy a cat condo. These are relatively small, round, and carpet-covered, and have upper and lower compartments. When you're in the pet store aisle, just walk right by these things. They're often not sturdy and, because they're so small, your kittens will outgrow them in a few short months. The carpet covering doesn't inspire cats to scratch there anyway, so it can't be used as a scratching post. Kittens need climbing surfaces and great places to play as they learn about their emerging physical skills. Even with kittens, you're better off buying a good cat tree—you may find the kittens prefer it to your expensive living room drapes.

WINDOW PERCHES In rooms where you don't have space for a cat tree, or if you're limited by budget, window perches are another way to add vertical territory. Many perches don't require permanent installation and can be attached through tension-mounting and/or hand-tightening screws without damaging your walls. That's great news for apartment dwellers.

Window perches come in various coverings. Some have removable covers that can be machine washed. There are a few perches that have heating elements as well, so your kitty can stay toasty warm while bird-watching on even the coldest day. The heated perches are wonderful for arthritic or elderly cats, but for cats who have trouble jumping, you'll have to provide easy access to the perches.

Window perches come in various shapes and styles. Some are padded flat-board styles, and others are designed like hammocks. When shopping, keep your cats' preferences in mind based on the types of places you've seen them sleep in the past. Some cats like the cozy comfort of a hammock, but others may feel too vulnerable and would prefer some solid support.

Even if you have cat trees, it's a good idea to have at least one window perch because it creates a middle level for the hierarchy. The perch is also very portable, so if you have to set up a sanctuary room temporarily (see chapter 4) in order to introduce a new cat or reintroduce a resident kitty, it can be used in there.

CATWISE TIP

If some of your cats are jumping on the counter, get a package of Sticky Paws and some cheap plastic place mats. Sticky Paws is a double-sided transparent tape that comes in strips (available at pet supply stores). Place strips of the tape on the place mats, then lay the place mats on the counter. This form of "remote control" training allows the cats actually to self-train as they quickly decide the counter isn't such a fun place to be. Keep the place mats on the counter whenever you're not using it until the cats are trained. Remember, though, provide other elevated areas for them.

HIDEAWAYS Your timid cats or ones who are low in the hierarchy may seek out the hiding places in your home. If you do have cats who like to hide, it's good to have options for them in every room. You can use A-frame beds that look like little padded tents for the cats who like the security of knowing no one can sneak up behind them. Place these beds in secure areas that are out of the main flow of traffic, and make sure the occupant of the bed can see what's happening in the room so he has adequate warning to escape.

Since most cats don't prefer sleeping directly on the ground, you may also want to consider the hammock-style beds with frames that can be connected. The frames enable you to put more than one bed side by side at varying heights. You often find these beds through mail-order companies.

TUNNELS These are wonderful for playing in and also as secure passageways for frightened cats.

For playtime, a tunnel is a great place for a cat to hide as he waits to pounce on a toy during your interactive play sessions (see chapter 5). Cats love hidden areas where they will be "invisible" to potential prey. Tunnels are also terrific during social play between companion cats.

For the frightened cat, a tunnel can provide a secure way to get from one side of the room to another. When I set up a sanctuary room for a cat, I often create a few tunnels: one from a hiding place to the litter box and one to the food bowl. The tunnel doesn't have to go right up to the litter box or food bowl; it mainly just needs to cover the center of the room, because that's where the cat will feel most vulnerable and exposed. This may encourage a frightened cat to feel secure enough to start venturing around the room.

You can be as elaborate and creative as you want when it comes to tunnels. You can buy soft-sided cat tunnels that connect to make them long and winding, or you can make several short tunnels. Soft-sided tunnels are available through mail-order companies and in some pet supply stores.

Another option is to make your own tunnels so they can be customized for specific areas of your home. When creating a tunnel, cut out one or two escape holes along the sides. This way, if two cats enter the tunnel from opposite directions, they won't meet each other head-on, and one cat can escape out of the hole to avoid a feline train wreck.

Tunnels can be placed just about anywhere. If you don't want them to be so obvious, you can slide your couch out from the wall a bit and place the tunnel behind it. Just leave enough room between the wall and the tunnel so the escape hole can be used.

If you want your cats to have some tunnels but you don't want to spend any money, you can make a tunnel out of paper bags or boxes by cutting out the bottoms and taping the ends together. If using paper bags, roll a cuff several times over on each end to prevent the bags from collapsing. Don't forget a couple of emergency escape holes. You may not think the box or bag tunnels look very attractive, but your cats will have a blast.

CAT-ACCESS STAIRS AND SHELVES If you still feel your cats don't have enough vertical space, consider creating a mini stairway connected to the wall that leads to a walkway near the ceiling. You can make this look very architectural and modern, so people will think you did it as a work of art. No one has to know it's for the cats.

I was recently a part of a project for Friskies cat food in which we designed the Ultimate Cat Habitat to help educate owners on how to create a more enriching indoor environment for their cats. The habitat was designed and created by Frank Bielec (the designer from the TV show *Trading Spaces*), Lou Manfredini (Mr. Fixit on the *Today* show), and me. Among the many cat-inspired elements we designed was a cat stairway along one wall that led to a catwalk. The walkway went around part of one wall and ended up at a multiperched cat tree. Cats could access the walkway from either the tree or the stairway. The stairs and walkway were painted to match other colors in the room, and the overall effect was very aesthetically pleasing. When we unveiled the Ultimate Cat Habitat at the Atlanta Home Show, many people who weren't even cat owners commented on how much they liked the idea of the stairway. Perhaps they were thinking of it for plants or knickknacks. With a little creativity, you can enrich your cats' environment in a way that's pleasant for you and enjoyable for them.

If you do a catwalk, make sure there are at least two ways to access it so one cat won't be able to trap another. It's a good idea to make sure a cat ascending one side can see if another cat is ascending at the other end. This way he can opt not to continue up the stairs if he doesn't want to chance an encounter.

LAST BUT NOT LEAST Finally, keep in mind that when it comes to territory, there is no issue more sensitive than the litter box. Where you put the litter box and how many boxes you have are two underappreciated and yet extremely crucial aspects of multi-cat ownership. (This topic is covered in depth in chapter 7.) As with the litter box, where you put the scratching post and how many you have becomes a critical territory issue with multiple cats. (This subject is covered in chapter 8 along with a brief refresher on what types of posts to choose.)

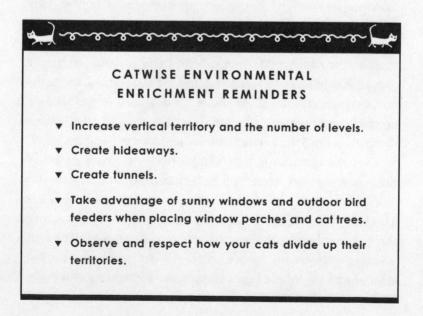

CATWISE ENVIRONMENTAL ENRICHMENT REMINDERS

▼ Increase vertical territory and the number of levels.

▼ Create hideaways.

▼ Create tunnels.

▼ Take advantage of sunny windows and outdoor bird feeders when placing window perches and cat trees.

▼ Observe and respect how your cats divide up their territories.

INDOOR TRANSITIONS

If some or all of your cats have outdoor access, and you want to make the transition to having them all indoors exclusively, it's not as hard as you may think.

The outdoor environment is not a safe place for a cat. There are so many dangers out there, including cars, disease, poisoning (accidental or intentional), injury or death from cat fights or other animal attacks, parasites, getting lost or stolen, and indiscriminate mating. Keep your cats indoors and you'll know they're safe. They can still enjoy indoor versions of all the good aspects of outdoor life through environmental enhancements and interactive playtime.

Additionally, from a behavioral standpoint, outdoor access can elevate tension because a cat may come back agitated by the scents of unfamiliar cats in his territory or maybe from actually having an encounter. The outdoor environment is unpredictable, and giving your cats access to it can bring unknown and unwelcome stress into your home.

It will provide wonderful peace of mind to know all of your cats are safely indoors and protected. At the start of the transition it can be very helpful if you're heading into winter. The cats probably spend more time indoors anyway, so that'll speed things up a bit. Start keeping the kitties in longer and longer.

Even though your indoor/outdoor cats may have all lived in the house together, there will be a change when everyone stays indoors permanently because their territories will be reduced. The loss of the outdoor home range may cause the cats to go through a period of renegotiating territorial boundaries and working out new time-share schedules. To help with this, look around and see where you can increase some vertical territory with an added cat tree here or a window perch there.

If the previously indoor/outdoor cats were outside for much of the day, you'll now have more litter box usage. You may have to increase your daily scooping schedule, and you may even have to add a box.

Be forewarned that at least one of the cats will not view this indoor transition as a good thing. You can pretty much count on at least one kitty sitting by the door and meowing in his most insistent tone. He'll look over at you with confusion, wondering whether you've lost your mind or maybe you just can't *hear* him—so he'll meow even louder. Do not let him out under any circumstances. No matter how loud and persistent he gets, don't give in. If you crumble, you'll be setting yourself up for failure, because the next time he wants out he'll meow and cry, knowing that it worked last time.

You can save yourself from much of the meowing and crying with behavior modification. You can use the *diversion technique* (described in chapter 5) to redirect his attention before he actually starts crying. Since he's a creature of habit, you can observe and anticipate the movements and behaviors he goes through before he actually sits and cries at the door. He might walk a certain way or go outside immediately after eating, or he may scratch on the post closest to the door. The nanosecond he gives you one of those early cues, that's the time to redirect his attention. I know you can't be watching his every move twenty-four hours a day, but the more often you catch it, the sooner you'll break the behavior pattern.

PROVIDE ADEQUATE STIMULATION One of the things cats love about being outdoors is the opportunity to hunt. If you're going to transition your cats indoors, you'll have to make sure they remain active. Get on a schedule of interactive playtime with a fishing pole toy at least twice a day. Interactive playtime, as

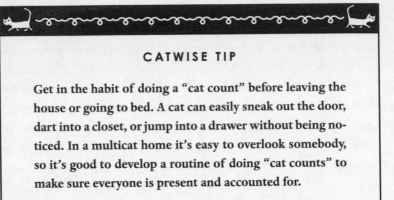

CATWISE TIP

Get in the habit of doing a "cat count" before leaving the house or going to bed. A cat can easily sneak out the door, dart into a closet, or jump into a drawer without being noticed. In a multicat home it's easy to overlook somebody, so it's good to develop a routine of doing "cat counts" to make sure everyone is present and accounted for.

described in chapter 5, will allow a cat to be the Mighty Hunter without the risk of disease or parasites from real prey. It'll also mean you'll no longer have to deal with a dead or, worse, an almost-dead mouse dangling from a cat's mouth as he trots into the house.

Since the outdoor environment would also provide your cat with the opportunity to climb, leap, explore hiding places, or just lounge in the sun, this is the time to make some of those indoor environmental modifications if you haven't already. Invest in good scratching posts, create some tunnels, and place a cat tree by a window. Play a cat entertainment video that showcases wildlife such as squirrels, birds, and butterflies. Cats love these videos, and you can find them in pet supply stores, through mail-order companies, and online.

Another outdoor attraction is grass. Cats love to nibble on grass. Even indoor cats love it, and that's why some of your cats may be munching on your houseplants. You can provide safe greens in the form of wheat, rye, or oat grass. Pregrown "kitty greens" packages can be found in pet supply stores, but you can also grow your own from seed planted in potting soil. Keep the container in a sunny location, and, when the grass gets long enough, offer it to your cats. To prevent squabbling, grow a few containers of kitty greens and place them in various locations. Most houseplants are poisonous to cats. To keep your cats from munching on houseplants, spray the leaves with a bitter apple antichew spray made especially for plants. These products are found in pet supply stores.

New Introductions

Because cats are social and territorial, introductions require a little finesse, a lot of patience, and let's not forget the all-important ingredient: bribery! Even though a new cat introduction may take some work on your part, it's a small amount of time given what the reward will be—cats who learn to coexist peacefully and, in most cases, form close relationships.

While there are many people who may brag about how they just "tossed" the cats in together and let them work it out for themselves, I'm here to tell you that's absolutely, positively, no-doubt-about-it the worst thing you can do. Unlike dogs, cats are not pack animals and are not quickly receptive to newcomers. The biggest mistake I find owners make is not preparing ahead of time. It's only after the fur is flying that they realize there's a problem, and then they have to begin the process of damage control. No matter whether you are adding a second cat to your household or your seventh cat, there is no introduction shortcut. Do it right the first time, and you'll save yourself and your cats much grief.

This may be ridiculously obvious but stop to consider if it is appropriate to add another cat to your household. Will this be a benefit or detriment to your current feline family? Do you feel all the cats will have adequate territory? Are you able to dedicate the time and patience required to do an introduction? Even when a new cat takes you by surprise, such as in a rescue situation, you should still set up a game plan that will cause the least amount of stress to everyone concerned.

If you are dealing with any sort of litter box problem—whether it's inappropriate elimination or spray-marking—get it resolved *before* you add further stress to the situation by introducing another cat. If your cats have a litter box problem now, it'll turn into a bigger one when the newcomer arrives. See chapter 7 for help in resolving litter box issues.

THE SANCTUARY ROOM

When you bring a cat into a new home, it is absolutely necessary that she have her own safe little sanctuary room. The newcomer needs a quiet, safe area where she can get her bearings, and the residents don't need to have a new cat immediately in their faces, intruding upon their territory.

The sanctuary room gives the newcomer an opportunity to get familiar with the scents of her new home. It also gives her time to get to know you and begin the trust-building process. For a rescued cat who has been through a physical or emotional trauma, a sanctuary room enables her to make the transition in a calm, comforting way.

A sanctuary room can be any room in your home that has a door. The cat doesn't need a lot of space right now—she needs safety and security. Even if your cat won't have any other pets to deal with, a sanctuary room is still needed. Think of how overwhelming it would be for a little cat to try to get comfortable and find her way around a home. She isn't going to remember the location of the litter box in time to take care of business or where she last saw her food. This is especially overwhelming and unfair to a kitten, who needs a convenient setup since her litter box habits are still in the learning stage. If you're bringing in an adult cat, you have to consider the stress factor as well. You don't want your new cat spending the first couple of months hiding behind furniture or under the bed because she is too threatened to get her bearings.

PREPARING THE SANCTUARY ROOM

The first rule is that the room shouldn't be empty. There's nothing more frightening for a cat than not having a place to hide. It's important to set up additional hiding places so the cat doesn't just dive under the bed if you're using a bedroom and stay put for weeks. Boxes are simple and effective hiding places. Put one or two on their sides and line them with towels or T-shirts that contain your scent. If the cat is truly terrified, use the boxes, or paper bags, to make tunnels for her, as described in the previous chapter. Make sure the size of the box and the holes you cut match the size of the cat. Soft-sided fabric tunnels also work.

Place the food and water bowls on one side of the room and the litter box on the opposite wall. The litter box shouldn't be located close to the food because cats don't eliminate where they eat. No matter how small the sanctuary, make sure you've separated the food from the litter box as much as possible.

The litter box should be uncovered. If you're bringing in an adult cat and she had a previous home, try to use the same type of litter she's accustomed to and then gradually transition to the kind of litter you use with the rest of your cats by mixing in a small amount of the new litter into the current brand, slowly increasing the amount over the course of several days.

DUST OFF YOUR CAT-PROOFING SKILLS Look around the sanctuary room with a fine-tooth comb and do some serious cat-proofing. Secure dangling electrical cords, remove delicate knick-knacks, and make sure lamps aren't top heavy. Use cord shorteners for the cords on venetian blinds, and so forth. If the newcomer is a kitten, coat electrical cords with a bitter apple antichew cream.

Plug in a night-light so you won't have to flick on a bright light when you enter the room to check on the cat. This will be especially important if you're dealing with a rescued cat or one who is very frightened in the new surroundings.

FRIENDLY PHEROMONES If the newcomer is an adult, use Feliway in the room. This is a behavior modification product that contains synthetic feline facial pheromones. Cats facially rub where they feel comfortable, and the scent helps them feel reassured and calm. Specifics about Feliway can be found in chapter 7. Feliway comes in a plug-in diffuser and a spray bottle. If you use the spray bottle, you'll have to spray every twelve hours. For the sanctuary room, I'd recommend you use the diffuser because you'll make your life so much simpler—it lasts about a month and covers approximately 650 square feet.

SCRATCHING The sanctuary room will need a scratching post. This is not only important so the cat can condition her claws and stretch her muscles, but it's comforting for a newcomer entering unfamiliar territory to be able to see her claw marks and recognize the scent left by the pheromones in her paw pads. If you're adopting a kitten, it's also important to have a scratching post in the sanctuary room so she can get a good head start on appropriate training.

Don't use one of the scratching posts currently in your home in the sanctuary room. Your newcomer doesn't need to be overwhelmed by the markings and smells of the other cats right off the bat. Also, you want to cause minimal disruption to your resident cats, so moving one of their posts would not be a good idea.

You can read chapter 8 to determine what type of scratching post to use in the sanctuary room. I'd recommend a tall, vertical post covered in sisal and also a horizontal scratching pad. For the horizontal pad you can get an inexpensive corrugated cardboard scratcher—cats love them. Since you probably won't know whether the newcomer has a preference for horizontal or vertical scratching or both, you'll be covering your bases and protecting your furniture.

TOYS You'll need some toys for the cat to enjoy during solo object play and at least one interactive fishing pole toy. The interactive toy will be an important tool for building trust so you can keep your distance while the cat learns to associate you with positive experiences. Interactive playtime techniques can be found in chapter 5.

For solo toys you can get a couple of furry toy mice and some crinkly balls at the pet supply store. The Play-n-Squeak mouse is also a great choice. Choose appropriate toys for the cat's age, size, and temperament. Don't get huge, intimidating toys for a kitten or a frightened cat.

EXTRAS Cats love and need elevated perches, so add a window perch or a cat tree to the room if you can. At the very least, put a cat bed on top of a box or piece of furniture or lay a couple of extra pillows or folded towels on the bed.

If the room you're using as the sanctuary has a VCR or DVD

player, you can play cat entertainment videos or DVDs. The new-comer will think she's staying in a luxury hotel.

LIMITED SPACE CONSIDERATIONS If you don't have a bed-room, den, or other regular-sized room to use as the sanctuary and must turn a bathroom into one, make necessary modifica-tions to create a hideaway and a sense of security for the cat. Per-haps a cat bed or a folded towel can be placed in a box on the counter or in the sink. Just do the best you can with whatever space you have.

PREPARING THE REST OF YOUR HOME

Let's start with litter boxes. You may need to increase the num-ber of them in your home. Even if you're going from just one cat to two, that doesn't mean they'll share a box. If you have sev-eral cats, adding another kitty may throw off the litter box bal-ance, so keep an eye on things and be ready to up the number of boxes and their locations if needed. Ideally, you should have as many boxes as you have cats or at least as close to that as pos-sible. The addition of a new cat is also a good time to install a cat tree or window perch, especially if you are going from one cat to two.

CAT-PROOFING Even though you may have adult cats who no longer play with cords or knock things over, that may not be the case with the newcomer, especially if she's a youngster. To be safe, just as you did in the sanctuary room, go through your home and secure dangling cords, coat electrical cords with a bit-ter apple antichew cream, make sure window screens are secure, and move breakable items to more secure locations.

THOSE FRIENDLY PHEROMONES AGAIN Just as Feliway may help the adult newcomer feel more comfortable, those pheromones will benefit the cats on the other side of the sanctuary room door. Be sure to spray around the sanctuary room door or plug in the diffuser if you have outlets in that area.

PRE-INTRODUCTION VETERINARY CHECKUPS

Your veterinarian should see the newcomer before you bring her into your home. She should get all appropriate tests and, if needed, be vaccinated and dewormed. The veterinarian will also check for parasites such as fleas, ticks, and ear mites because you certainly don't want to introduce those little critters into your home. Depending upon your case specifics and the health of all the cats involved, your veterinarian can make a recommendation on how long you should quarantine the new kitty and whether she needs to be retested before exposure to your resident cats.

Make sure all your cats are up-to-date on vaccinations. If you don't vaccinate some or all of your indoor cats due to age or medical concerns, don't bring an unfamiliar cat into the environment without first checking with your veterinarian and taking the necessary safety precautions.

THE INTRODUCTION PROCESS

The big day has finally arrived. Bring the cat (in her carrier) into the home and go right to the sanctuary room, which you will have already set up. If the cat is an adult, open the carrier and then leave the room. This way, she can stay in the carrier until she feels comfortable enough to start investigating the room and won't be intimidated by your presence. Have food and water set up for her, although she probably won't be interested in eating right away. She may, however, appreciate that the litter box is so conveniently located. It's good to leave the newcomer alone for a while so you can concentrate on your resident kitties, who may or may not be aware of what just took place. When you leave the room, don't overcompensate for the situation by cuddling excessively or your cats will really be convinced that something big is up. Be as casual and as normal as possible.

If the newcomer is a kitten, you may want to spend a little time with her before leaving the room to make sure she knows where everything is located.

Keep a robe in the sanctuary room during the initial stages. This way, you can hold her without getting an overwhelming amount of her scent on you. Be sure to wash your hands afterward as well. Even though your cats will surely be able to detect the smallest amount of the newcomer's scent on you, there's no need to present an in-your-face insult when you go to pet one of your resident kitties.

Use this initial separation time to do interactive play sessions with the cats. Do your regular play sessions with the resident cats as usual. If one or two of the cats hang out by the sanctuary door and appear upset, you can conduct an interactive play session right there and then gradually entice the cat away from the door. You can't keep the cats away from the door (and actually, you do want them to start investigating), but by doing play sessions, you may be able to keep a kitty from camping out at the door and getting very upset.

Interactive playtime with the newcomer is an important trust-building exercise to start immediately. If the newcomer is a kitten, the playtime will help her bond with you and also help her work off some of that endless kitten energy. If the newcomer is an adult, especially if she's frightened, the interaction will help her stay within her comfort zone while playing. This is a great way to build trust.

There are two important aspects to the introduction process that I want you to remember. The first is that the process must be done *one sense at a time,* and the other is that *you must give the cats a reason to like each other.* Mere separation is only half the process. You can keep cats separated for months, but if you don't help them form positive associations with each other when they do finally meet, the introduction is likely to fail.

By one sense at a time, I refer to how the cats will first smell or hear each other before they see or touch each other. Scent will play a big role in this process, and your cats' noses will really be working overtime. By restricting the process to one sense at a time, emotions stand a much better chance of staying in control . . . relatively speaking.

Once the newcomer is in the sanctuary room, you may need to leave things at this stage for a while before progressing. Your cats may already be upset over the fact that someone's on the other side of the door. You need to let them get used to this and give the newcomer time to get situated. Use your best judgment concerning the time to start actively introducing the kitties. You know your cats better than anyone else, so you should be able to tell when it's okay to proceed. For example, your cats should be on their normal routine (for the most part), willing to play, and not redirecting aggression toward companion cats. The newcomer must be secure and comfortable as well before beginning or else she'll just spend all of her time hiding. There is no set time for how long introductions should take. Every cat is an individual, and every owner's set of circumstances is different. Some cats can breeze through this process in a matter of days, and others take weeks or even months. Don't be discouraged if your in-

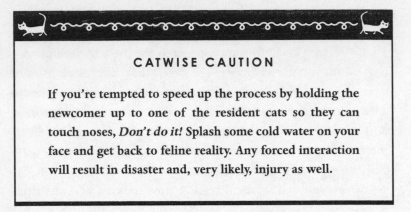

CATWISE CAUTION

If you're tempted to speed up the process by holding the newcomer up to one of the resident cats so they can touch noses, *Don't do it!* Splash some cold water on your face and get back to feline reality. Any forced interaction will result in disaster and, very likely, injury as well.

troduction takes longer than the one your neighbors did for their cats. My best advice to you is to let the cats set the pace.

THE SOCK EXCHANGE The first sense to introduce is scent. The sock exchange will help the newcomer and residents to begin to get to know one another in a very safe, controlled way. Pheromones are scent chemicals that tell a lot about a cat to others. This sharing of information of the friendly facial pheromones is a great first "how do you do."

Take a few pairs of socks and put one sock on your hand. Now rub one of your resident cats gently along the cheek to collect some facial pheromones. Use a different sock for each cat so you don't cause tension. If you have a large cat community, don't rub everyone at the same time. Start with the one or two you feel will be most receptive to the new cat. Choose a sociable but calm cat to prevent intimidating the newcomer. This will come in handy later because you'll be introducing those cats first.

Once you've collected the scent on one sock, go into the sanctuary room and, with a clean sock, rub the newcomer around the face if she's comfortable enough to allow it. Leave the resident's sock in the newcomer's room and take the newcomer's sock into the main part of your home. If the newcomer is frightened or you feel rubbing her cheeks will damage any trust building you've already done, then don't worry about it. You can just place a couple of clean socks in one of her beds and, after she has been lying on them, take those out to the main part of the house for the resident cats. Don't use anything bigger than a sock. You don't want to overwhelm anyone with something as big as a scented towel.

The sock exchange can also help you determine how upset or calm a particular cat may be. If a cat goes crazy and starts hissing, growling, and attacking the sock, chances are this will not be a record-breaking introduction in terms of speed. If the cat sniffs the sock and shows only mild interest, that is a good sign. Even if a cat does show a strong negative reaction to the sock, don't be discouraged. Introductions are tough in the beginning, but that's not necessarily an indication of how the cats will ultimately get along. It's normal to experience a bumpy road at first, and it's much safer to let the cats work out their "concerns" on the sock rather than each other.

Do the sock exchange several times a day until you feel every one has become somewhat familiar with one another's scent.

THE ROOM EXCHANGE To begin, put the resident cats in a separate area of the home so the newcomer can safely start to become familiar with a larger territory without fear of being ambushed. As she moves around the house she'll also deposit more of her scent, which will help your resident cats adjust to her ever-increasing presence.

When you let the newcomer out of the sanctuary room for the exchange, just open the door and let her walk out on her own so she'll know the sanctuary room is right behind her if it's all moving too fast. Don't pick her up and drop her in the middle of the living room because she'll probably be frightened and will just end up hiding. If she starts to look nervous, you can use an interactive toy to entice her. If she's food motivated, offer a treat as she ventures out.

It's now time for your resident cats to check out the newcomer's territory. Obviously you'll have to make sure the newcomer is safely in another room. Depending upon how many cats you have and their personalities, you should start with the one or two kitties most likely to accept the newcomer. One thing to watch for when doing a room switch is *redirected aggression*. If one of the resident cats gets too upset, she may lash out at a companion cat, which is why it's important to be careful about which cats you let into the sanctuary room initially. It may be better to do it one at a time. Also, don't just dump a resident cat into the sanctuary room; rather, open the door and let her decide how far and fast she wants to go.

If you live in a small apartment and there aren't enough rooms to do this, you may want to enlist the help of a family member so you don't have to play cowboy to a herd of cats. If you live alone, ask a cat-loving friend or neighbor to help. You can put the newcomer in her carrier and have the neighbor take her out of the apartment temporarily while the kitties check out the sanctuary room.

After the room exchange, reward your cats with a meal or a treat. Always end these training sessions on a positive note. Keep the sessions short. What's most important is the newcomer's discovery of the main part of the home. It isn't as crucial that the resident cats explore the sanctuary, so if they get upset, don't continue it.

Do this a couple of times a day until you feel the cats are comfortable or at least getting comfortable with one another's scents. It might take just a day or it might take several. Again, let your cats set the pace.

PLEASED TO MEET YOU Okay, now that everyone is getting comfortable with new scents, it's time to let the cats see one another. Their exposure should be brief, positive, and at a safe distance. Remember one of the rules I mentioned earlier: *You must give the cats a reason to like each other.* Open the sanctuary room door and let the cats see one another while everyone is offered a treat or a meal. Make sure to offer the newcomer and residents their treats on opposite sides of the room. You may have to pull out all the stops here and use something truly delicious and irresistible. When using cat treats, break them into small pieces so you don't interfere with regular nutrition. The cats will still view it as an extra-special treat. If your cats don't like the commercial treats, you can use small pieces of shredded cooked chicken. Another sure-fire favorite is meat or chicken Stage 2 baby food. Get the pure meat or chicken without any additives. Don't get Stage 3 food because they tend to contain onion powder and other things that cats shouldn't eat, and the texture isn't as smooth and appealing. Again, use just enough to entice them. If you give them treats too frequently or too abundantly, they won't hold the same power over your kitties.

If they're really food motivated, you can feed their meals in the presence of one another. Place the bowls on opposite sides of the room. You want to show the cats that good things happen when they're in one another's company. If some of the cats aren't food motivated, you can use interactive toys as a form of diversion. If one cat gets too focused on another, you can shift her attention to the toy. It's okay if the newcomer chooses to stay at the far end of the sanctuary room. End the session immediately after everyone has had a snack or a few minutes of playtime. It's better to do several thirty-second sessions that end positively than to force the cats together for a half hour and end the session unexpectedly with hissing or growling. I know it's tempting to keep a session going longer because the cats seem to get along, but remember there will be time for that later. It's worth taking the extra time now to do things right in order to set the kitties up with the best chance of being friends. In the beginning, be conservative.

Periodically, take the tiniest amount of soiled litter from the newcomer's litter box (use no more than one-eighth teaspoon to start) and place it in one of the litter boxes that the resident cats use. Don't use more to start with or you'll risk creating a litter box aversion problem. Then take a tiny amount of soiled litter from one of the main litter boxes (again, no more than one-eighth teaspoon) and place it in the newcomer's box. If the cats show a negative reaction, back off and next time use an even smaller amount.

MAKING PROGRESS When the cats can interact for longer periods of time (an hour or more), keep the sanctuary set up because you'll want to put the newcomer back in there at night and when you're not around to supervise. As for supervision, keep it casual in appearance so the cats don't feel as if you're hovering over them. You want to see their reactions, and they may not act as naturally if you're too close. Some cats feel more secure when the owner is nearby, so you'll have to create a balance: present but casual and relaxed.

If you sense too much focus on the newcomer or growing tension, toss out some treats or a toy to divert them. Anything that will be viewed as positive to shift their mind-set will work. Keep an interactive toy nearby to use if you notice one cat starting to stalk another, and try to use it *before* an actual incident

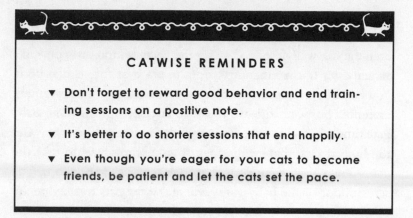

CATWISE REMINDERS

▼ Don't forget to reward good behavior and end train-ing sessions on a positive note.

▼ It's better to do shorter sessions that end happily.

▼ Even though you're eager for your cats to become friends, be patient and let the cats set the pace.

occurs. In a pinch, if one cat is about to attack another, you can make a loud noise or clap your hands, but the more you can keep things positive, the faster the cats will accept one another. Don't get upset or punish any of your resident cats for showing aggres-sion. This will only undo the positive associations you're trying to establish.

Watch for subtle threats. A direct stare and raised hindquar-ters is an easy posture for owners to miss but is most intimidating to a new cat. You may want to put bells on the collars of the cats who consistently display aggression so everyone can better mon-itor their whereabouts.

Whether the introduction takes days, weeks, or months, don't get discouraged. You have to go at the pace that suits the cats. You may find some phases of the introduction go smoothly, but then you'll hit a snag. That's normal, so just try to hang in there.

WHAT TO DO IF THINGS AREN'T GOING WELL Sometimes a newcomer may have trouble leaving the safety of the sanctuary room. If that's the case, try slowing down the introduction. You may be exposing the cats to one another for too long a period or you may have rushed through one phase of the process. If things aren't going well despite slowing the pace, temporarily put up a screen door to the sanctuary room in place of the regular door. You can buy inexpensive screen doors at a home improvement store. If you want to leave the regular door up, get three baby gates and put them in the doorway—one on top of another. Get the hinged kind that swing open so you won't have to take the gates down every time you want to enter or exit the room. The screen door or the baby gates will allow the cats to see one another and have closer contact yet still remain safe. They will, we hope, start to become desensitized to one another's presence. This method isn't needed in most cases, but you might feel safer taking this middle step before going to unrestricted access.

THE NEW SPOUSE OR SIGNIFICANT OTHER

Many times cats like the new spouse (then you'll just have to work on your mother's opinion), and you all can become one big happy family, but what about when things don't go so smoothly? What if one or more of your cats hate the love of your life?

TREATMENT PLAN Even if your cats liked your spouse while you were dating, a full-time living arrangement can be another matter altogether.

If you and your cats plan to move into your spouse's home or a new home, follow the instructions in this chapter under "Introducing Cats to a New Home."

If your new spouse and his or her furniture are moving into your home, try to make the transition gradually. Start incorporating the unfamiliar furniture into the home a few pieces at a time and spray the corners with Feliway. If you are planning one big move, bring over smaller pieces in your car before the actual moving day. The more gradual you can make the transition for your cats, the easier it will be. It's also important to maintain your cats' schedules. If they're used to specific times for play sessions or meals, don't deviate from that.

One thing to know about and plan for in advance is your spouse's reaction to living with cats. Does your spouse have an allergy to cats? Does he or she have strong feelings about where the litter box should go? About kitties lounging on his or her furniture? If one or more of your cats sleep with you at night, how does your spouse feel about that? Talk about these issues in advance so they don't later escalate to a crisis level. If you decide it would be best to start locking the cats out of the bedroom, it'll be much better to begin that transition before the spouse moves in. You certainly don't want your cats making the negative connection of being locked out with the arrival of the new person. Start keeping your bedroom door closed all of the time so your cats get out of the habit of wandering in there during the day. You'll be decreasing territory by closing off that room, so increase it with cozy cat trees, perches, and hideaways in other rooms.

Now, what if some of your cats hate your spouse? The first rule is that he or she mustn't try too hard to be the cats' new best friend. While it's important that they develop positive associations with the new spouse, it's also crucial that the cats, not your spouse, determine the pace. See the next page for some tips.

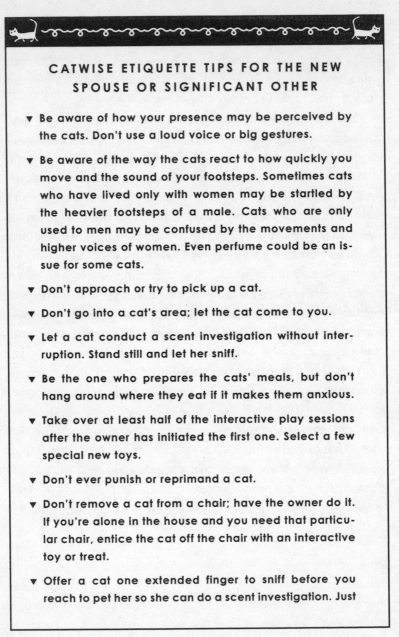

CATWISE ETIQUETTE TIPS FOR THE NEW SPOUSE OR SIGNIFICANT OTHER

▼ Be aware of how your presence may be perceived by the cats. Don't use a loud voice or big gestures.

▼ Be aware of the way the cats react to how quickly you move and the sound of your footsteps. Sometimes cats who have lived only with women may be startled by the heavier footsteps of a male. Cats who are only used to men may be confused by the movements and higher voices of women. Even perfume could be an issue for some cats.

▼ Don't approach or try to pick up a cat.

▼ Don't go into a cat's area; let the cat come to you.

▼ Let a cat conduct a scent investigation without interruption. Stand still and let her sniff.

▼ Be the one who prepares the cats' meals, but don't hang around where they eat if it makes them anxious.

▼ Take over at least half of the interactive play sessions after the owner has initiated the first one. Select a few special new toys.

▼ Don't ever punish or reprimand a cat.

▼ Don't remove a cat from a chair; have the owner do it. If you're alone in the house and you need that particular chair, entice the cat off the chair with an interactive toy or treat.

▼ Offer a cat one extended finger to sniff before you reach to pet her so she can do a scent investigation. Just

> hold it still and let her come to you. It's good cat eti-
> quette that's similar to the nose-to-nose greeting used
> by familiar cats when they meet. Show your good cat
> manners and you will know by her reaction if it's okay
> to proceed.

BLENDED FAMILIES

It's not only about *his kids* getting along with *her kids.* It's also about *his cats* getting along with *her cats*—not to mention dogs, birds, the guinea pig, and the twelve-year-old son's pet tarantula.

One of the hardest hurdles a blended family has to face in terms of the pets concerns how to introduce the cats (okay, sleeping under the same roof with a tarantula may be high on the hurdle list as well). The situation can be made easier if you follow a few basic rules.

TREATMENT PLAN If you are moving to your new spouse's home, then *your* cats should be put in the sanctuary room. Slowly help the kitties get to know the new human family members and then proceed with a new cat introduction. This is a huge transition for your cats, so they need as many allies as possible. Cats hate change, and a new home, a new human family, and new cats rank high on the cat stress-o-meter. If your spouse is moving into your home, then *his or her* cats go into the sanctuary room.

If you are all moving into a new home, there are some benefits to that from a cat's point of view. The new home is neutral territory that no cat has claimed yet. Set up two sanctuary areas. A move to a new home is stressful in itself, so, just as you would do in a typical new cat introduction, let the cats get comfortable in the sanctuary room before proceeding. Let each set of cats out separately to explore the house a little at a time. To determine whose cats should go out first, if one spouse's cats tend to be more frightened, then those are the cats who should have the first exposure so they won't be initially intimidated by the scents deposited by the other kitties. After the cats seem calm in the sanctuary area and have checked out the rest of the house, you can start the actual introduction.

INTRODUCING CATS TO A NEW HOME

Talk about change! It doesn't get much more overwhelming than this from a cat's point of view. Cats take great comfort in the familiarity of their surroundings. Introducing cats to a new environment can be seriously upsetting.

Your cats have worked out a hierarchy in your current home and established individual personal territories within it. It may have taken some of your cats quite a bit to negotiate their little corner of the world. To them, the move to a new home feels as if a giant came along and shook up the world, and their things landed in all the wrong places.

TREATMENT PLAN As you prepare to move, spray Feliway on the corners of the boxes you bring in before packing. Even though cats normally love boxes, it may be stressful to have so many strange-smelling boxes in their home, especially as their environment starts to change once packing gets under way.

You should have sanctuary rooms set up in the new place before the cats arrive. How well your cats get along and how many you have will determine how many sanctuary rooms you'll need. Be sure to match together cats who get along even under stress. Put familiar furniture in the sanctuary, but if you're separating cats into various rooms, try to match cats with their favorite pieces of furniture. You don't have to put pieces of furniture in the sanctuary room that belong in other rooms, but just be aware of little touches that can create security.

Try to keep the surroundings as familiar as possible. For example, don't go out and buy new furniture all at once if you can help it. Your cats will take comfort in finding their favorite pieces of furniture even if they're not all in the location they remember. If you normally keep throws or afghans on your furniture, don't launder them right before moving. Being able to detect their familiar scents will provide more security for your cats.

Even though you'll probably be exhausted and overwhelmed yourself by the move, take care to keep your cats' daily schedule. The more they can hold on to that's familiar, the better. Don't neglect those daily play sessions—your cats need them now more than ever! Help your cats develop positive associations with the new home by conducting games in various rooms.

Despite all the stress of moving, you may find an unexpected bonus. Because a new home is neutral territory, some of the cats who didn't get along previously might now get along. The territorial divisions may have changed enough to make more of the cats feel secure, especially if you've moved to a larger home. You may also find that the hierarchy may shift a bit, especially among the middle-ranking cats.

BABIES AND CHILDREN

Cats and kids can form wonderful and close bonds, but some preparation is needed to help kitties adjust to this major life-changing event. Many people mistakenly believe that cats retaliate out of jealousy when a baby enters the family. This is totally false. Any behavioral changes that occur, such as elimination outside of the litter box, for instance, are as a result of the stress and anxiety caused by confusing circumstances. Remember that *cats hate change* and that *cats are territorial creatures of habit.* So imagine the stress of suddenly finding that there's a hairless, strange-smelling, very loud little creature in your home. On top of that, your owners are no longer acting normally. Nobody consulted the cats about this change, so they often find themselves overwhelmed with stress.

When you have more than one cat, you may find that with the arrival of the baby, the dynamics between the cats change. One may become more anxious when the baby comes home, and that can trigger some of the others to then get anxious. It can create a chain reaction of anxiety because the nervous cat is no longer acting normally. That confuses her companions. The cats who may initially get the most stressed out are the Velcro kitties—the lap cats who are most bonded with you. Because you're spending so much time with the baby and maybe aren't keeping up with the normal kitty rituals, they become confused. They may become more vocal or start eliminating on your bed or on clothing left on the floor in order to combine your scents. While this soothes the eliminator, the scent of urine in inappropriate areas will also probably cause the other cats concern. When you have more than one cat, it's not just the cat with the behavior issue you have to address—you also have to be aware of how that cat's behavior affects the rest of the group.

TREATMENT PLAN The best solution is to plan ahead so the cats aren't faced with the sudden shock of a new baby. Start by doing nursery preparations well in advance so you can go gradually. If you're going to convert a room that some of your cats currently use, start getting them used to other places. If you have a cat tree in that room, move it to another very appealing location. Take time to play with your cats at the newly located tree to get them comfortable with this change, and be aware of territory rights when you move the tree. Since you'll be decreasing horizontal territory, make some vertical increases. This will also come in handy later when the cats will want places to get out of the baby's reach.

Do the nursery decorating gradually to give your cats time to adjust to all the different scents. Don't paint, wallpaper, install new carpet, and bring in the new furniture all in one weekend. This is especially crucial if one of your cats tends to stress out if you buy so much as a new footstool.

Even if you don't mind if the cats come and go in the nursery, the one place you want to make sure they don't camp out on is the crib. There's no truth to the ridiculous myth that cats steal the breath from babies, which probably began as a way of explaining what we now know as sudden infant death syndrome (SIDS). However, since a newborn baby is unable to turn, you don't want anything in the crib anyway—not even a blanket. Because some of your cats may view the empty crib as a great place to nap, start the training process right away. Get a bunch of empty soda cans and plastic bottles. Make shake cans by putting a couple of pennies in each can and taping over the opening. Put pennies in the bottles as well and then recap them. Fill the crib with the cans and bottles so the cats can't find a comfortable place anywhere. Keep the cans and bottles in place until the baby comes. If you do it early enough, the cats will make the association that the crib isn't such a great place to be. After the baby comes, if you're still concerned about a cat jumping in there, you can buy a crib tent. The Cozy Crib Tent is very strong, even under the weight of a cat, and you can find it online and probably in some baby stores as well. I wouldn't rush out and buy it until you see if you need it. It was my experience as well as many of my clients' that the best cat deterrent in the crib is the ear-splitting noise emanating from the wailing baby herself.

To help cats get used to the scent of the baby, the mother-to-be should start wearing baby lotion and powder. Another good way to help your cats become familiar and comfortable with scents associated with a baby is to start washing your family's clothes in baby detergent. Since baby detergent is formulated to get out tough baby food stains, you'd be surprised at how well it works on the rest of your family's laundry.

When preparing my cats, I also found it helpful to buy and play with some of the larger and noisier baby toys in advance so they'd have time to get used to the often-startling sounds they make.

If your cats have never been around babies, you should start exposing them gradually by inviting friends with babies over for short visits. Make the visits brief and as low stress as possible. Timing will be important because you don't want the friend to bring the baby over when she's due for a nap and might be cranky. You can also ask your friends if they'd record some baby sounds for you, especially crying sounds. Play the tape at a low volume while you conduct interactive play sessions.

One big mistake some owners make is that they shower their cats with an unbelievably large amount of attention before the baby comes, thinking this will help ease the stress afterward. This actually backfires because the parents can't maintain that level of attention after the baby arrives, and the sudden decline in what the cats have come to expect as normal increases stress. It's better to establish a realistic schedule before the baby comes home so you'll be able to maintain it afterward.

If you don't already have cat trees and elevated perches for your cats, don't delay any longer. Get those things well in ad-

vance of the baby's arrival so your cats have time to get comfortable with them. When the baby starts crawling, the cats need areas of escape. You may think you have plenty of time before the
baby is mobile, but, trust me, it's easier to find the time to shop
and help the cats adjust before you're a new parent.

This is also the time to start making litter box adjustments.
The boxes will have to be relocated out of the way of a curious
baby. Move the boxes gradually to avoid litter box rejection problems. Any boxes that are to be relocated should be moved a few
feet a day until they're in the desired areas. Also, keep territorial
considerations in mind: which cats use that box most often, and
will it go into an equally secure area?

If the baby has arrived and some of the cats aren't handling it
well, you can still make things better. One of the things you
shouldn't skimp on is the interactive playtime. Try to maintain
the twice-daily schedule. You'll even get coordinated enough to
where you can hold the baby and maneuver a fishing pole toy. If
I can do it, you can do it. If there are other family members available, enlist their help with play sessions when you're busy with
the baby.

Even if you can't interact with your cats physically because
you're feeding, changing a diaper, or playing with the baby, you
can interact with them verbally. Use a soothing tone of voice to
talk to them. Mention their names often and describe what
you're doing. You may find that the combination of hearing their
names and perhaps being able to rub against you or curl up near
you as you feed the baby will be very comforting.

Watch for preliminary warning signs that a cat is getting upset
or fearful around the baby. Don't wait for the cat to strike out,
and distract her at the first sign of potential trouble. It's best to
catch behaviors early and divert them so the cat doesn't begin to

associate the presence of the infant with being terrified. Put bells on the cats you're most worried about so you can better keep track of their whereabouts.

As your baby grows, it'll be important to teach her how to interact gently with the cats in a positive way. When babies first learn to touch, they tend to grab with the subtlety of a sledgehammer, and that won't go over too well with your cats. Start early and be consistent in teaching your child how to pet gently with an open hand. Hold your child's hand to prevent her from grabbing and making a fist, then gently stroke the cat. You'd be surprised how early that message of gentleness can be conveyed to the child. It also helps your cats become used to the child's touch and know they can trust it.

Don't ever let your child tease your cats, and teach her as soon as practical to become familiar with feline body language. Also, teach the message about off-limit times and places. For example, cats are to be left alone when eating, sleeping, using the litter box, and hanging out in their perches or cat trees.

If a cat who normally gets along with a particular child suddenly starts acting aggressively or terrified, one of the things you need to investigate is the possibility of abuse. While in many cases a child hurting a pet is accidental, there is a possibility of intentional abuse. Children who abuse animals are usually very secretive about it, so you have to be observant of the relationship between your children and your cats.

INTRODUCING YOUR CATS TO A DOG

Just when you think you've gotten the stress in your feline household down to a bearable level, a cute little puppy comes into your life. Suddenly the cats are diving under the bed or leaping onto the highest perches in the house.

A dog can be a wonderful addition to the family, but you need to plan to teach her how to interact with the cats in a safe and comfortable way.

Cats and dogs can be terrific companions, but it's important to get everyone started off on the right foot. Dogs and cats speak different languages, and you need to help them find common ground. Although you won't have the same territorial issues to deal with as when you bring a new kitty into the house, you will have to work on social etiquette. Dogs and cats have different ideas on how to play, and that can cause problems. Dogs play by chasing and play wrestling. Your cats may run, and the dog will interpret that as an invitation to play. The more the cat runs, the more the dog chases. This sets both of them up for continual frustration because the frightened cat will be conditioned to run every time she spots the dog.

As a pack animal, a dog also doesn't understand the protocol of feline greetings. Take a dog to the park, and, chances are, within minutes she'll find another canine buddy. Two cats will never be friends in the space of a few minutes. The trick is to help the dog learn how to approach.

TREATMENT PLAN Here's how a basic training session should go. The dog should be on a leash and the cats should be loose in the room. You may want to do the first few sessions with just one cat—the most potentially dog-friendly one. Have some dog treats in your pocket and a couple of dog toys. Have a friend or family member sit on the other side of the room with the cats to help distract them and keep them relatively relaxed. The goal of this session is to get the dog to focus on *you* as the leader. Start with the dog seated. Offer her a toy; when she relaxes and focuses on you or the toy, offer a treat. If she stands up and tries to move toward one of the cats, give a slight correction with the leash to get her focus back on her toy or on you. When the dog responds, offer a treat immediately. You can also use clicker training during these sessions. Click the second the dog does what you want, then offer a treat. She'll soon connect the sound of the clicker with the forth-coming treat. Clicker training can be helpful because it immediately lets the dog know what you want from her. As you proceed through these sessions, you can gradually inch closer to the cats. These sessions will show the dog that cats are neither toys nor prey to be chased. They will also help the cats realize that the very sight of the dog doesn't mean they're in danger.

It's important to have a well-trained dog under any circumstances, but with cats in the house, you have to make sure everyone feels comfortable and safe. If you're unsure whether you can trust the dog with the cats, consult an animal behaviorist or a qualified dog trainer. Never leave the dog and cats unsupervised until you're absolutely sure they have established a safe relationship.

Environmental adjustments may be necessary when a dog joins the feline family. Litter box locations need to be secure so the dog can't ambush a cat in the litter box. You may even discover that the dog visits the litter box for something to munch on. It seems completely gross to us, but dogs frequently seek out solid feline waste. If you find that to be the case, block the doorway to the litter with a baby gate—your cats can still enter but the dog can't. Place a sturdy box on the other side of the gate so the cats have something to jump onto if they're reluctant to jump the top of the gate. If you have a large dog, you may be able to raise the gate a few inches off the ground so the cats can scoot underneath.

The feeding station is another area that may require some adjustments. If you previously had ground-level stations, you may

CATWISE CAUTION

An introduction that should never be attempted is between cats and their natural prey. If you have a pet snake, bird, caged mouse, or gerbil, and so forth, *do not* allow the cats access to where these pets are kept. A cat is a predator, and even if you have a very secure cage setup, it's *extremely* stressful for the caged pets to live with that constant fear.

need to elevate them all or relocate the food to rooms where the dog is not allowed.

Cat trees and elevated perches will also be needed—the cats need safe places for retreat. If you have a very large dog who can access the taller perches, train her that the trees are off limits.

5

Let's Play!

To understand how cats play, you first have to understand how they hunt. Cats don't hunt by engaging in long chases. A cat is a sprinter and doesn't have the lung capacity to chase prey to exhaustion. His skill is his stealth. For a cat, the hunt is as much mental as it is physical. It isn't just luck that's involved in being a successful predator—it takes planning, speed, and accuracy. A cat hunts by silently scouting the area, alert to any sound, scent, or movement that might indicate potential prey. When the cat spots the prey, he uses his exquisite stealth to stalk the target, inching closer and closer. He uses any available object for cover such as a nearby tree, bush, or a rock. His body and head are low to the ground. Whiskers and ears are in the forward alert position. The unsuspecting prey goes about its business as the cat efficiently closes the gap. When the predator gets to within striking distance, the cat pounces on the prey with lightning speed. If his aim is good, the prey will instantly be killed by a well-placed bite to the spinal cord. This is referred to as the "killing bite."

CATWISE ALERT

Adult cats don't engage in social play unless they're with familiar social companions. Otherwise, the play can easily cross over into aggression.

Your approach to interactive play should be to simulate a hunt. You want to make this mental and physical stimulation as realistic as possible for the cat, short of bringing in a live mouse. A good way to become more familiar with beneficial play technique is to observe how a cat actually hunts. Watch your cats track a bug in the house or go after a toy mouse. Watch television programs that show how big cats hunt. You'll need to understand what movements stimulate cats the most and how they react if you want the play session to have a positive effect.

There are two main types of play: *object play,* where a cat plays with a toy, and *social play,* where a cat plays with another animal (usually another cat). Interactive playtime is a variation on object play, but you control the toy's movements. Your cats will engage in solo object play (where they bat toys around on their own), and they may also engage in social play with one another. Both of these are important, and interactive play can be a very powerful behavior modification tool.

Interactive play requires a fishing pole toy. This type of toy is valuable because of the following:

 * You can move it like real prey.

 * It keeps a safe distance between your hands and the cat's teeth.

* It allows a frightened cat to decide how much personal space he needs, so it's a great trust-building tool.

* The cat doesn't have to "work" to make the toy come to life the way he does with his other toys.

Since you're controlling the toy's movements, the cat can shift into predator mode and enjoy the game. Believe it or not, many owners don't play correctly with their cats, and that can lead to a disinterested, overstimulated, or frustrated cat. If done correctly, interactive playtime can not only be a fun experience for the kitty and for you, it can also help you correct a behavior problem.

You should use interactive play in two ways. First, you need to set up a daily schedule for maintenance sessions. Don't let the word *maintenance* fool you, though. You'll look forward to these sessions, too, as a form of laugh therapy as you watch your Mighty Hunter stalk that elusive mouse. The second way you'll use this playtime is for on-the-spot sessions in response to specific be- havioral issues. The daily maintenance sessions will help you pre- vent behavior problems from cropping up in the first place. They also provide the necessary mental stimulation that predators need as well as exercise to keep your kitty healthy. No kitty tread- mills will be needed at your house. It's a great way to prevent boredom, combat depression, and alleviate stress. Here's my little secret: An interactive play session is one of the best ways I destress as well.

You'll use the on-the-spot play session to diffuse a tense sit- uation between cats, help a frightened kitty to change his asso- ciation with a particular area or a particular cat, and help a cat remain positive after a traumatic experience.

Even if you currently enjoy play sessions with your cats, if you aren't doing it on a daily basis, you may not be supplying them with the amount of activity they need. You're also missing out on a lot of fun yourself. In a free-roaming environment, an exceptional feline predator would probably hunt down and capture about ten mice or other small prey a day. That's a lot of activity. Now, imagine your kitties. How much daily activity are they engaging in? Don't count being chased by another cat, because I'm referring to positive, confidence-boosting activity.

The truth is that even though kittens seem to be able to play endlessly, many adult cats fall into the couch potato category. Since these feline couch potatoes gradually become less and less active, many owners don't really notice the change until the annual veterinary exam when the cat is diagnosed as overweight. "Overweight? My kitty? How did that happen?" That's when many owners come to the realization that the cat's only physical activity consists of the walk from the couch to the food bowl.

When you think of the benefits of daily play, compare it to an exercise regimen that you might have. If you engage in activity only sporadically, it doesn't benefit you as much as if you exercised on a regular basis. Doctors repeatedly advise us to do a little something every day. The same applies to your cats. Ideally, you should try to do two fifteen-minute interactive play sessions every day with your cats. This chapter shows you how to conduct both individual and group play sessions, so if you have many cats, you won't have to quit your job to stay home and entertain your kitties. If you don't have time to play with them all every day, choose the ones who seem to need it the most that day. If two cats who have a good social relationship have been romping around quite a bit, you can skip the daily play session for them. If you can squeeze in a play session for everyone, that would be sensational. Your kitties will love it.

MOUSERS, BIRD-WATCHERS,
SPIDER SNATCHERS, AND CRICKET NABBERS

One reason to get a variety of toys is because a cat is an oppor-
tunistic hunter, and he never knows what prey will become available. The technique the cat uses to catch a bird will be slightly
different from the one used to capture a little snake. Although
the basic concept of stalking and pouncing are the same, the cat
must adjust for each individual hunt. If you provide a variety of
interactive toys, you give your cats the opportunity to test their
skills. We all like a little variety. One note though—you'll probably find that your cats will develop a favorite toy. If that's the case,
you'll know which one to use when you need to distract that
kitty. If you do have a cat who wants to play with only one particular toy, that's fine, but periodically keep trying other toys as
well. You may find that once he gets into a routine of the daily
play sessions he'll be receptive to other "prey." Start out by buying one, though, so you can first let your cats test-drive it. When
you know a toy is a hit, then buy a second one for group play.

One final, but very important note on interactive toys: They
should be stored in a safe place. Never leave these toys out because the cats could chew and swallow the strings or get tangled
in them. Also, you want to keep the toys special, and if you leave
them out, they'll lose their appeal. Leave out safe toys for object
play—such as the furry mice that always end up under the refrigerator. Store the interactive ones in a cat-proof closet. You may
even need to rotate where you store the toys or you might find
your cats sitting and staring at the closet door. Interactive playtime is *that* powerful.

TOYS THAT SAY "WOW"

You may have a basket filled with toys for your cat, but they are really dead prey. In order to make them come to life, the cat has to do all the work. An interactive toy is based on a fishing pole design. There are numerous kinds available but you'll want to use toys that you'll be able to move like prey. Almost all of the toys I mention can be found at many pet supply stores, through mail-order companies, and on the Internet.

Da Bird is an outstanding toy that consists of bird feathers attached to a swivel on the end of string, which hangs from a pole. When you move the toy through the air, the feathers whirl around so it looks and sounds like a bird in flight. Talk about the "wow" factor; this toy has it. It should be a mainstay in your interactive toy collection. I've seen Da Bird cause the most hardcore couch potato to sit up and take notice.

Another terrific toy is the Cat Dancer. It's made up of a long wire that has very tightly rolled-up heavy-duty paper rods attached to the end. It may not sound great, but trust me, this toy is a big hit with cats! With just the slightest movement from you, the toy bounces and jerks all over the place. It's similar to the erratic movements of a fly. I'm sure you've seen how crazy your cats get whenever there's a fly loose in your house. The Cat Dancer is especially effective for cats who are high energy and very athletic. (Any Siamese owners out there?) The erratic movements inspire stop-on-a-dime precision and spectacular leaps from your Super Kitty, and it's very inexpensive.

Another wire-based toy that packs a lot of "wow" is the Dragonfly. This consists of a Mylar dragonfly on the end of a thin, flexible guitar-string wire. The wire is so thin, all the cat concentrates on is the dragonfly itself. There's a wooden handle on the other end for you, so the toy is very comfortable, and its lifelike moves are outstanding. My cats go crazy when it hovers in one spot just inches above the ground. When the toy moves, the Mylar wings make an irresistible sound. When I use this toy, I have as much fun as the cats. Each Dragonfly cat toy is handmade and well worth the price. See the Appendix for ordering information. Another great feature of the Dragonfly and the Cat Dancer is that they're excellent toys if you have limited play space because you don't have to contend with a long wand.

For cats who like snakelike movements, the Swizzle Teaser tops my list. Don't worry, if you don't care for snakes yourself, this one is cute. It is a soft, furry snake with a feathery tail. Sounds kind of weird, but it's very enticing to a cat as it slides around the corner out of sight or wiggles along the carpet and up in the air. This toy is a favorite of my cat Mary Margaret. It's a quiet toy, so it's great if you don't want to attract other cats into the room while you conduct a private session with a specific kitty. The feathery end piece of the Swizzle Teaser is attached with Velcro so you can change it for another type of "tail," which is a great way to provide some variety. Also, if you don't secure the Velcro too tightly, then your cat can truly "capture" his prey.

The toys mentioned above are just a few of the numerous interactive toys available, but they're truly exceptional. When you go shopping for toys, keep two things in mind: Match the toy to your cat's age, ability, and hunting preference. Make sure you can move this particular toy in a preylike manner. There are so many great toys out there that I'm sure you'll be able to find something every one of your cats will love.

PLAYTIME WITH PIZZAZZ

First, we have to create some atmosphere. Since cats hunt by hiding and then stalking, look around the room and make sure there

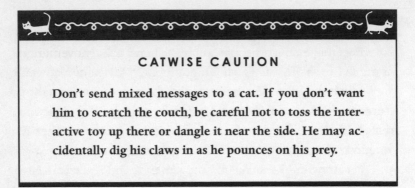

CATWISE CAUTION

Don't send mixed messages to a cat. If you don't want him to scratch the couch, be careful not to toss the interactive toy up there or dangle it near the side. He may accidentally dig his claws in as he pounces on his prey.

are places for a cat to hide. If you're going to play in a big open room, put a couple of boxes or open paper bags in the middle of the floor for the cat to use as cover.

If you want to play with just one cat, do it in a separate room so you don't drive the other cats crazy. Perhaps do the session when the others are napping, or pop in a cat entertainment video for them.

Okay, now let's get down to the nitty-gritty of the technique. The secret is to move the toy like prey. The biggest mistake owners make is to dangle the toy in the cat's face. Although the cat may paw at the toy, it's not the way he would naturally hunt, so you won't be triggering that important mental part of the hunt. If you're doing playtime to boost kitty's confidence or relieve his stress, the mental aspect is as important as the physical.

The other big mistake I see owners make is that they wave the toy frantically around and make the cat go on a marathon run. This is just physically exhausting for the cat and also very frustrating. Even if you have an overweight kitty who needs to shed a few pounds, exhausting him to the point of heart failure isn't the way to do it.

If you're going to move the toy effectively, keep a couple of things in mind. First, you want this to be a positive, confidence-boosting experience, so make sure the cat has several successful captures throughout the game. Second, vary your movements so you really are simulating prey movement.

In order to move like prey you'll have to think like prey. What would a mouse do if he found himself in your house? He'd scurry around and dart from one hiding place to another. He might hide behind the leg of a table and peer out to see if the coast is clear. Our "mouse" might also dash under the couch and quiver. For a cat, it's just as exciting when the prey stops moving for a moment, hides, or quivers. It's at those times that the cat can plan his next move or prepare to pounce. Just try it and you'll see for yourself: have it peek out from around a corner or out from under a piece of furniture. If you're using the Dragonfly,

CATWISE TIP

If you have a timid cat who might initially be intimidated by an interactive toy, you can start by doing a low-intensity session using something as simple as a string attached to a pole. Use a very strong, safe string like the ones attached to interactive toys, and be watchful that your cat doesn't chew it. As the kitty gets more comfortable you can then start to introduce the other toys, but keep your movements gentle.

It'll also be helpful for a timid cat if he can sniff and investigate the toy before the session. Place the toy on the ground, and let him check it out.

one of the most enticing moves is just to have it hover a few inches off the ground the way a real dragonfly might.

Another very important technique is to move the toy *away* from the cat. Remember, no prey in its right mind would head *toward* the cat. Wiggle the Swizzle Teaser away from a cat or have it lazily curl around a doorway out of sight and watch how it sparks a cat's interest. As your cat's prey drive is stimulated and he goes into action, take a moment to observe what a beautiful, intelligent, graceful athlete he is.

If you're using Da Bird or a similar flying toy, you should alternate between in-the-air movements and on-the-ground movements. It's while the bird is on the ground that the cat will pounce.

You may find that some of your cats don't enjoy air hunting, while others go absolutely bonkers for it. If you realize that you have cats who prefer strictly to ground hunt, then adapt your technique accordingly, or use a different toy. It won't take long before you'll be very familiar with the types of toys or movements that are irresistible to each cat.

DON'T FORGET THE SOUND EFFECTS Very often, the sound of a mouse scurrying through the grass or a chipmunk hiding in the leaves will be what first alerts the cat. Don't worry, I'm not going to tell you that you have to squeak like a mouse or chirp like a bird—although if that helps you to "think like prey," then go for it! I'm actually referring to the enticing sounds a toy makes on different surfaces. Take the toy and have it make a "scratch, scratch, scratch" sound by rubbing it against the side of a box or bag. If you use the Dragonfly or Cat Dancer, have the "prey" dart inside a paper bag that's on its side and then tap or rub the toy against the sides. It probably won't take long before your cat dives headfirst into the bag. Even the sound of the toy skittering across a floor can spark a cat's interest.

GOTCHA Because you want this to be a positive, fun experience for your cat, let him successfully capture his prey several times during the game. In a real hunt, the cat might catch the prey between his front paws, where it might stay, wriggling to get away. Do that type of movement with the toy as well. If the cat grasps the toy and holds it down with his front paws, let it sit there for a few seconds and then gently start to wriggle it free. The cat has small whiskers on the underside of his front paws that are used to detect even the slightest movement of trapped prey.

AND THE WINNER IS . . . The one thing you don't want to do is leave your cat revved up at the end of the game. If you suddenly just stop playing and put the toy away, you'll leave the cat

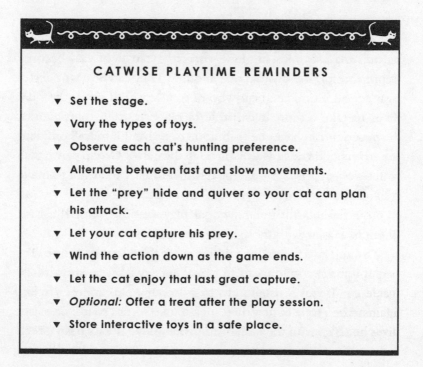

CATWISE PLAYTIME REMINDERS

▼ Set the stage.

▼ Vary the types of toys.

▼ Observe each cat's hunting preference.

▼ Alternate between fast and slow movements.

▼ Let the "prey" hide and quiver so your cat can plan his attack.

▼ Let your cat capture his prey.

▼ Wind the action down as the game ends.

▼ Let the cat enjoy that last great capture.

▼ *Optional:* Offer a treat after the play session.

▼ Store interactive toys in a safe place.

in an excited state. From his point of view the hunt may not have been over. When you know you want to end the game, wind the action down gradually, almost as if the prey is injured. If you're using Da Bird, keep the movements on the ground, maybe as if the bird has a broken wing. This will enable your cat to have one final grand capture. Then, if he's food-motivated, you can offer him a treat. Winding down will help your cat settle back to normal. Having satisfied both the mental and physical aspect of his prey drive, he'll be more likely to be relaxed.

If you don't want to give treats to your cats, you can schedule the play sessions before dinner so the cats experience a hunt before the feast. If you leave dry food out for free-choice feeding, freshen up the food and water after a play session.

GROUP SESSIONS

Group play sessions, if done correctly, can help cats become more comfortable around one another. They can be a wonderful way for an intimidated cat who normally would sit on the sidelines to take a more active role in playtime. This only works, however, if you have the technique to prevent a more confident cat from bulldozing his way through the game. Group play is also a time-saver if you have a large number of cats and want to make sure they all get their playtime.

You should still do individual play sessions with the cats, though, at least with those kitties most in the need.

Group play can be done with two or three cats at a time. Try to combine cats who are of the same energy level or who already get along. If you're using a group session to help cats learn to like each other a little better, then stick to two kitties so it'll be easier for you to control the situation. If one of your cats hasn't been active in a long time or is stressed or extremely timid, he'll need individual sessions for a while to build up his confidence before he is ready to play in a group.

To start, you'll need two interactive toys. Hold a toy in each hand. It'll be easier if you choose two of the same type of toys so your movements will be more coordinated. It may seem very awkward at first, but you'll get better with practice. I can hardly walk and chew gum at the same time, and I can handle two toys very easily. In the beginning, you may find it easier to use the shorter-handled toys such as the Dragonfly or Cat Dancer.

You want to use two toys so the cats aren't competing. If several cats are all focused on a single toy, they'll become more concerned with watching to see who'll pounce first, and the game will no longer be fun. Competing for one toy can also intensify a timid cat's fear because he won't take the chance of pouncing and risk getting attacked by another cat.

Basically, the concept is that the cats will be playing *near* each other but not necessarily *with* each other. Cats who have a good relationship may learn to play cooperatively with one toy, but why create potential conflict when, with just a little more effort, you can create a positive, comfortable playtime environment. As you're playing, if one cat loses interest in his toy and eyes the other cat's toy, slow the movement of the popular toy and increase the action on the other toy to refocus the cat's attention. With a little practice you'll have this technique down to a fine art and will look like a maestro conducting the orchestra. Of course, enlist the help of friends and family members. Why should you have all the fun?

THE DIVERSION TECHNIQUE

Here's a scenario: One of your cats is sitting on the cat tree or window perch, looking out the window peacefully. Another cat enters the room, spots the other cat, and assumes that low-to-the-ground, slinking posture associated with stalking. The cat at the window remains unaware that he is about to be ambushed. What do you do?

Previously, you may have yelled at the stalking cat or chased him out of the room. Although your motives were good, these methods scare the innocent cat as well and keep both cats in a negative state of mind. A more positive option would be to divert the aggressor's attention with an interactive toy.

For the diversion technique, any interactive toy will do, but I particularly like the Dragonfly and the Cat Dancer because the wire can be curled up for easy storage. That means you can stash a toy in a drawer, hide it under a couch cushion—anywhere it's convenient to grab in a hurry. In my house you can get your hands on a Dragonfly or Cat Dancer within seconds no matter which room you're in. It works best to keep a few of them stashed in rooms where the cats tend to hang out. The next time you see a cat about to cause trouble, quietly and quickly grab the toy and divert his attention away from the intended victim. The sight of the toy will trigger his prey drive, and you'll be shifting him into a positive mind-set. Conduct an on-the-spot mini play session, and he'll forget all about the other cat.

The great thing about the diversion technique is that even if you misread the cat and he wasn't about to cause trouble, he got a bonus playtime out of it, so there's no harm done. If you had chased him or yelled, it would've left things on an unnecessarily negative note.

Now, of course you can't always be in the room when two cats are about to go at it. There will also be times when you won't see the behavior until the aggressor is too close to the targeted cat or they've already locked eyes on each other. The key to the diversion technique is timing. You need to get the cat's attention before he gets too focused on his target. If you notice the problem too late and the cats are already in a struggle, then make a

noise to startle them. Then, once the two cats have run their separate ways, get a toy and casually (being casual is important here)
offer the attacked cat some low-intensity playtime to help get
him out of that frightened, negative state. If he's really upset after a serous fight, then leave him alone to calm down. Never
physically try to break up a fight.

The diversion technique can be applied to other situations as
well. For example, if one of your cats is still adjusting to indoor
life and cries at the door to go outside, divert his attention to an
on-the-spot play session before he gets to the door or starts crying. Fortunately, because cats are such creatures of habit, you
should be able to pick out his pattern rather quickly. This can also
help a timid cat who dives under the bed whenever company
comes over. This technique is covered in depth in chapter 10. Another use is when one of your cats is spray-marking. In addition
to following the instructions in chapter 7, divert his attention
when you notice he's backing up to an object or walking toward
a favorite spraying target. There are so many uses for the diversion technique. Think of it the next time you want to change a
cat's negative state of mind to a positive one.

THE GRAVEYARD SHIFT

If you live with several cats, there's a pretty good chance that
you've had at least one four A.M. wake-up call. Whether he wants
food, a place on your pillow, or just a bit of playtime, a cat can be
mighty persistent.

If you've been getting up to put food in his dish when he sits
on your chest at four or five A.M., then you're reinforcing his behavior. Even if you try to hold out as long as possible before you
simply can't stand it anymore, every time you get up lets him
know his method worked.

Maybe your cat doesn't want food—he merely wants your attention. Out of frustration you may have resorted to locking him out of the bedroom. Although it may work with some cats, in other cases you may end up with having to listen to the endless sound of a cat scratching and pawing at the door or scratching at the carpet.

Cats tend to become more active after dusk. Just as you're winding down from the day, a cat is revving up. After engaging in several catnaps during the day, a cat is ready for play when the sun goes down. You also have to keep in mind that you've been gone all day, so when you come home at night, your cats are stimulated by your presence.

Fortunately, there's an effective and fun method for curbing nocturnal activity based on natural cat behavior.

Normally, you may come home, feed your cats, play with them, and then settle in for the night. Perhaps the cats curl up next to you as you read or watch TV. Then, it's off to bed. While this routine is great from a bonding/affection standpoint, it doesn't address the kitty's stimulation needs.

To shift a cat's internal clock, I think of the cat's most basic behavior cycle: *hunt, feast, groom, sleep.* Cats engage in the basic activity cycle multiple times in a day. First, a cat goes through the stimulating activity of the hunt. Once the prey is captured, the cat enjoys his feast. After the meal, a cat fastidiously grooms himself to remove any traces of the prey's scent. This important survival skill is done so the scent won't alert other prey or make the cat the target of a bigger predator. With a full stomach and his grooming duties completed, the cat is ready for sleep. Keep this cycle in mind to change the unwanted behavior. Do an interactive play session right before bed, in addition to any other play sessions earlier in the evening. Okay, that takes care of the hunt, and now it's on to the feast. If you feed your cat on a schedule, divide up his portions so you can include the prebedtime feeding without increasing his overall amount. After the meal, he'll very likely groom himself and settle in for the night. If you leave dry food out for him, take it up in the earlier part of the evening and put it back down at bedtime, topping the bowl with some fresh kibble. If you don't want to take the food up because of the other cats, then just make a big ritual out of topping off the dry food right before bed.

Even if your cat isn't food-motivated, you'll improve the chances of a restful night's sleep if you get on a schedule of doing prebedtime play sessions. These sessions may have to be a bit longer than the usual fifteen-minute play sessions, but it's worth a little extra time to ensure a good night's rest.

For those cats who seem to defy the need ever to sleep, set up some activities to keep them occupied at night. This can be several open paper bags on their sides, an empty tissue box with a toy inside, or an empty box cut out to be a tunnel. For food-motivated cats you can set out a couple of Play-n-Treat balls. (Don't use this toy if you have a dog in your home because of the risk that he might chew or swallow the balls.) Fill the hollow ball halfway with dry food. There's a hole in the ball so as the cat bats it around, a piece of kibble periodically falls out. Rotate toys so you can bring out some "new" ones in the evening.

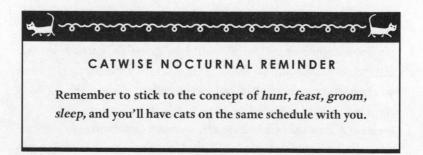

CATWISE NOCTURNAL REMINDER

Remember to stick to the concept of *hunt, feast, groom, sleep,* and you'll have cats on the same schedule with you.

Two of my cats love to patrol the house at night, so I strategically place toys for added enticement. I might place a furry mouse on the perch of a cat tree so that its tail hangs irresistibly off the edge. We have one toy in our house that's supposed to be a spider, but to me it just looks like a powder puff with legs. My cats go nuts for it, so at night I'll place it so the long legs dangle from a perch, or I'll hide it under the couch with a couple legs just peeking out. There's also a great little toy called Play-n-Squeak that my cats adore. It's a computer chip–activated toy mouse that makes an irresistible squeaky chirp every time the cat bats the toy. I vary what I do each night, and my cats look forward to the adventure.

CATNIP

Although catnip can be an asset in behavior modification, many owners either don't incorporate it into their cats' lives or they overuse it, which can leave cats immune to its effects. Here are the basics: Catnip contains a volatile oil that creates the "catnip effect." The effect is similar to that of an aphrodisiac, and catnip is safe and nonaddictive. Catnip is a hallucinogen that reduces a cat's inhibition and it creates a euphoric feeling that lasts about fifteen minutes. Cats may roll in, lick, or eat the herb. It shouldn't be left out all of the time because if cats are constantly exposed to it, they can become immune. Interestingly, the response to catnip is an inherited gene that about one-third of the cat population lacks. Catnip should be given only to adult cats. Kittens don't respond to the herb nor do they even need it, considering all their seemingly endless energy.

BENEFITS Catnip can help spark a couch potato to get off the couch and engage in a play session. If you're working with a cat who hasn't played in a while, catnip can be a great start. It's a wonderful tension reliever, so use it after your cats have had a stressful experience—for example, after you've had company or after you return from a trip. I give my cats a "catnip party" on days when I've had many behavior house calls and come home exhausted. I may be too tired to engage in a full interactive play session, but I want my cats to have a special time, so I sprinkle catnip on their favorite toys and rub some on the scratching posts, or I may fill a few socks with the herb.

Catnip is also a great way to help a frightened or timid cat come out of his shell. It's a wonderful start to an interactive play session for a kitty who is too timid to focus on the toy otherwise.

A COUPLE OF CATNIP CAUTIONS If you've never exposed a particular cat to catnip, it's a good idea to do it without the other cats at first. Some males may cross the line from play to aggression while under the influence of catnip. You'd want to know that before offering catnip to the whole group together.

HOW TO USE CATNIP You can grow your own, you can buy packaged dried catnip, or you can buy catnip-infused toys. If you grow your own, don't grow it outdoors if other cats can get into your yard or you'll be the most popular house on the block. If you grow your own, you can dry the catnip by hanging it in bunches upside down in a dry, dark place. After the herb has dried, strip off the leaves and blossoms (don't use the stems), and store in a tightly sealed container. Don't crush the leaves until you're ready to use the catnip because you don't want to waste it by releasing the oil prematurely.

If you buy packaged catnip, look for the brands that use only leaves and blossoms. Catnip that contains a lot of stems is of lesser quality. If the catnip is in a bag, repackage it in a tightly sealed container. When you're ready to offer the catnip to your cat, rub some between your hands to release the oils. You can offer the catnip loose or put some in a sock and tie a knot at the end. I also keep a few furry toy mice marinating in catnip. Rub some catnip on scratching posts periodically as well, if you're in the middle of training a cat to use the post.

Don't buy catnip-filled toys unless you know the quality of the manufacturer. Some catnip toys are filled with low-quality catnip, and some may not even be filled with true catnip at all.

In addition to offering catnip during times of stress or after a particular event, you can use it on a maintenance basis but not more than once a week.

Finally, keep catnip in a place the cats can't access. You'd be surprised at how determined a cat can be. I've heard of many plastic containers demolished by cats when owners inadvertently left them out on kitchen counters.

6
Mealtime

Mealtime can be a powerful behavior tool when trying to get cats to become friends, but feeding cats who are on different diets and who have individual feeding preferences can be extremely challenging. When you became a multicat owner, it probably didn't take you very long to realize that you needed an effective mealtime strategy. Those *single cat* days of placing a bowl of food on the floor and not having to worry about who did or didn't eat are over. There are, however, methods you can use to help make life a bit easier when those hungry little faces are all looking up at you in the kitchen.

BOWL PREFERENCES

Cats often have preferences when it comes to the type of dishes used for food and water. *What* you put the food into may not seem that important to you, but it could make a big difference to one or more of your cats. There are many choices out there when it comes to pet bowls. You'll find bowls in all styles and price ranges.

Plastic is a common choice for pet bowls, but I'd advise against it. Plastic tends to retain odor, and your cats may object to the old smells of previous meals. Plastic also scratches easily, and bacteria can get trapped in the tiny lacerations. Many cats can develop skin problems around the chin area (such as feline acne) from eating out of plastic bowls. Plastic is also very lightweight and can end up being pushed around the floor when your cats try to eat the last bit of food in their dishes.

Stainless steel is a great choice. It's virtually indestructible and easy to clean. To keep stainless steel bowls in place, choose the type with a rubber lip along the bottom. However, a few cats may object to the way certain moist foods taste in stainless steel bowls.

Ceramic is another great choice, and these bowls come in all colors and styles. Choose only U.S.-made bowls because ceramics manufactured outside of this country may contain lead in the glaze. Before buying a ceramic bowl, run your fingers over it carefully to make sure the surface is completely smooth. Any imperfections or rough spots can irritate a cat's tongue. Don't use a ceramic bowl once it has become chipped or you'll risk injury to a cat's mouth or tongue.

Glass is another option for food or water. If you choose this, just be careful when washing to prevent chips. Throw out any glass bowl that gets even the tiniest chip.

No matter how many cats you have, don't skimp on the dishes. Don't use old margarine containers or paper plates. Stainless steel or ceramic bowls are worth the investment because they'll last a long time.

Don't use divided dishes for food and water. Food particles can easily land in the water and contaminate it, making it less desirable to drink. Also, many cats prefer not to have their food too close to their water. If a cat is thirsty and not hungry, she may not want to have the smell of food so close by.

In addition to the preferences individual cats may have concerning what the bowls are made of, you also have to address bowl size. Some cats don't like having their whiskers squished or bent while eating, so they may prefer a wide, shallow dish. Long-haired or peke-faced cats also often prefer shallow bowls. Kittens don't want to drink out of a bowl the size of a swimming pool, and they shouldn't eat out of a trough that causes them to strain over the edge to reach the contents.

FREE-CHOICE FEEDING Most cats are nibblers by nature, so they do well by having the option of free-choice feeding. Most healthy, active cats don't tend to overeat, so leaving food available for them to eat at will is convenient for both cat and owner.

Free-choice feeding works best with dry food only because moist food becomes spoiled, hard, and unappealing if left out for more than a half hour.

With a multicat household it's not a good idea to have one community bowl. Even if all of your cats get along, there may come a time as they mature where territorial issues may come up, and one or two cats may start crowding others out. Tension between cats, anxiety, and hostility often extend to the feeding station as well. You want to create an environment where each cat feels safe enough to eat in peace. Set up more than one feeding station so one kitty doesn't have to cross into another cat's territory if there's hostility. If there isn't any hostility, you may be able to set up a few feeding stations in one area such as the kitchen. In a tense kitty household, though, you'll have to scatter them throughout the home. You may also have to create feeding stations on different levels. If there's a cat who doesn't seem com-

CATWISE CAUTION

Cats don't eat where they eliminate, so never set up a feeding station near a litter box.

fortable eating on ground level, she may need the security of an elevated feeding station. Another cat who is extremely timid may prefer a more hidden eating area, and if you have a dog or small children, you might need to place the bowls out of their reach. If you have a large cat population with a very dynamic hierarchy, put food bowls on various levels so the dominant, middle-ranking, and low-ranking cats all feel secure. Keep bowl preferences in mind when locating feeding stations. If you know particular cats have certain bowl likes or dislikes, make sure you allow for that when setting up multiple locations.

If you currently feed on a schedule and there's aggression or tension at the food bowl, or if a few cats are eating too fast, leaving dry food out for free-choice feeding may help. It will help the cats set up a more workable schedule of who eats when, and the multiple locations will ease territorial disputes. Also, the ongoing supply of food often discourages cats from gorging and then vomiting the food right back up.

SCHEDULED FEEDING

If you feed on a schedule, everyone should have his or her own food bowl and should be fed in the same position each time. With numerous cats that can be quite a challenge, but since they're creatures of habit, this routine can help create more security. Even if the cats don't stick to a particular bowl, by providing numerous bowls, they'll be better able to space themselves out. Cats who are not on the best terms will be able to maintain a socially acceptable distance, as will the higher-ranking and lower-ranking ones.

How far to separate the bowls will depend on the dynamics in the household. Some cats may be comfortable eating three feet apart while others may need to eat in a completely different room. A good rule to follow in general is not to place bowls up against the wall or in a corner, because some cats feel vulnerable with their backs to the entrance of the room. Slide the bowls out just a few inches so the more timid cats can keep an eye on the rest of the room. Scheduled feeding may also be made more peaceful by using levels. Some cats may prefer eating on an elevated surface.

One of the best ways to help cats start to form positive associations with one another is by having them eat while in sight of the others. However, adequate distance is very important so that each cat can remain well within her comfort zone. If a cat stops eating and starts looking at another cat, then it means the bowls are too close together. If you notice there's a problem with one cat becoming too possessive around the food bowl, or if some cats are afraid even to enter the feeding area or room, then separate feeding stations are needed. Try to put compatible cats together.

I know it makes meal preparation more work for you, but it's better to nip a behavior problem in the bud than to allow things to escalate into a feline food fight. Every cat should have total security while eating. If you're doing behavior modification to get certain cats to like each other, you can start by feeding in separate rooms and then gradually inch the bowls closer—but remember, let the cats set the pace on how close they want to be.

In many cases, if you don't have a large number of cats, en-

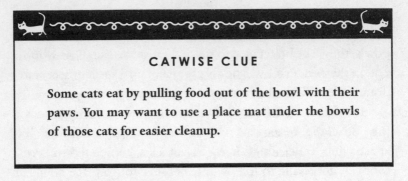

CATWISE CLUE

Some cats eat by pulling food out of the bowl with their paws. You may want to use a place mat under the bowls of those cats for easier cleanup.

suring security and making sure everyone eats out of his or her own bowl may just require your presence. Play security guard and help your cats find their designated bowls. If you're consistent, you may find that the routine will sink in and they'll head toward their bowls on their own in a short time.

If the possessiveness problem is very serious, or if one or more cats are remaining too nervous during mealtime no matter what methods you try, leave dry food out for free-choice feeding as well. The ongoing food supply may ease anxiety.

CATS ON SPECIAL DIETS

Oh boy, this isn't fun when you have more than one cat. This situation may arise if you bring a kitten into a household of adult cats. It can also be an issue if a cat must go onto a prescription formula due to a medical condition. Your veterinarian may also want one or more of your cats on a reduced-calorie formula due to a weight problem.

In some cases (for example, when dealing with an obese cat), elevating the regular food may prevent the dieting kitty from reaching it if her weight keeps her earthbound. This can also work with a kitten as long as she isn't able to climb to the food.

Most of the time, scheduled feeding is required when you have cats on special diets so you can be sure everyone is eating what they're supposed to. Depending on the particular diet and the age/health of your resident cats, you may be able to transition everyone onto the same diet. This is a decision your veterinarian should guide you through—don't make this determination on your own. If your cats have very clearly defined territories, you may be able to place the appropriate formula food in the specific cat's area.

For an overweight cat, it may help to feed her smaller meals more often. Her stomach won't be empty for such an unbearably long time, so she'll probably feel more satisfied. You can also leave out a few Play-n-Treat balls to help her get some added exercise, but make sure not to increase her total daily amount. Exercise the overweight cat with interactive playtime as well.

With a kitten, if she's getting close to her first birthday, is healthy, and is a good weight, your veterinarian may allow her to transition onto adult food a bit early. This may help if you've been struggling to keep your adults out of the growth-formula food, but don't make the early transition without the veterinarian's approval. Kittens need the extra fat and protein in growth formula.

THE PERIODIC NIBBLERS VS. THE "CLEAN PLATE" CLUB

If you're lucky, all of your cats are on the same page when it comes to eating style preferences. If you're not, you're probably scratching your head wondering how to satisfy the cat who takes two bites before walking away with the cat who eats until she sees her reflection in the bottom of the bowl.

Depending upon the athletic abilities of the cats involved, you may be able to put dry food on specific elevated surfaces for the nibblers in the group or place the food in specific territories. If that doesn't work, you can attempt to train the "clean plate" kitties to become nibblers by feeding smaller meals more often. Gradually make the meals smaller and more frequent so they get used to eating a few bites at a time. Leave Play-n-Treat balls out for them as well. The other option is to put all cats on scheduled meals. Feed frequently at first to get the nibblers used to a schedule. In time, they'll learn that the food is available only at specific times.

If possible, it's better to try to transition the cats to be nibblers (unless your veterinarian says otherwise) because it really is more natural for them.

FURRY THIEVES

With multiple cats, it often takes more of a concentrated effort when it comes to training everyone to stay off the counter. Even if you're feeding some of the cats on elevated surfaces, there are areas where you don't want your cats to have access—for example, the dining table and the kitchen counter. This effort becomes especially important if you hope to make sure nobody runs off with an uncooked piece of chicken or gets into the Thanksgiving turkey seconds before you're about to serve it to your company.

To keep cats off the counter or other surfaces, first determine where the cats will be allowed and not allowed. Make sure everyone in the family knows the rules as well because consistency is important.

Get some inexpensive plastic place mats at your local discount store. Also, get a package of Sticky Paws from the pet supply store. This product is a double-faced tape. You can also use regular double-sided masking tape if you prefer. Place strips of the tape on the place mats and then scatter the place mats on the counter. Use enough place mats so there won't be a comfortable place for the cats to land. You can also set up a few visual cues by placing some shake cans along the edge of the counter. (To make simple shake cans, put some pennies into empty soda cans and tape over the openings.)

This place mat method works well because it changes the cat's association with the area without involving you. Keep the place mats on the counter whenever you aren't using it. After a couple of weeks, start to remove them one at a time, leaving those closest to the front edge of the counter in place a little longer. Keep the shake cans on the edge of the counter the longest because the visual cue will remind the cats of how unpleasant the surface is.

If any of your cats are trash can raiders, get a can with a secure, locking cover. If your Houdini cats still manage to get into the trash, keep the can secured in a cabinet. If the cabinet door doesn't latch, attach a magnetic catch to the inside of it or use a child-proof latch.

Begging is another behavior you don't want to encourage. To correct cats who jump on the table during meals, keep a squirt bottle nearby that's filled with plain water. If a cat attempts to jump up, give her a quick spritz of water. Try to be sneaky so she doesn't see it's coming from you. If any of your cats beg, don't give in and offer table food. It not only upsets the nutritional balance, you can create a finicky eater if she decides she'd rather have your food than her cat food. If a cat begs, you can use the squirt bottle, but again, don't let her see that the correction came from you. If you feed your cats on a schedule, it'll probably help to feed them before you sit down for your own meal.

CATWISE CAUTION

Decide which elevated surfaces are off limits to your cats and remain consistent. Don't send mixed messages by allowing cats on the dining room table when there isn't food there but then shooing them off during meals. Provide appropriate elevated areas for your cats so they won't need to lounge on surfaces where food is prepared or served.

USING FOOD FOR BEHAVIOR MODIFICATION

Since most cats are food-motivated, the giving of a treat is often a very effective tool in behavior modification. Use treats specifically for training purposes, though. Don't just give them out for no reason. I know you love your cats and want to reward them, but providing top-notch nutrition, affection, playtime, and a loving and secure environment will more than make up for that daily treat.

When using treats for training, break them into pieces. Most cat treats are pretty generous in size, and if you break them into halves or quarters, you'll get more mileage out of them and you won't interfere with nutrition. During training, a cat needs only a small taste of this special treat and not a stomach full.

If your cats don't care for commercial treats, try some shredded cooked chicken. Again, only a small amount is needed. You can also try a spoon of plain yogurt or a tiny bit of meat or chicken baby food. If possible, though, stick to commercial treats so there will be no confusion between what you eat and what the cats are allowed to eat. There are many brands of cat treats out there in various flavors and textures, so, chances are, you'll find one that your kitties will love.

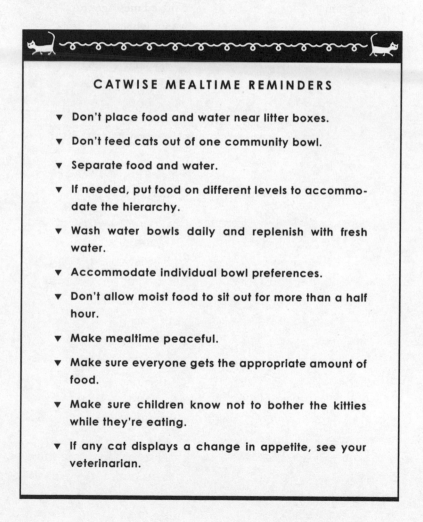

CATWISE MEALTIME REMINDERS

▼ Don't place food and water near litter boxes.

▼ Don't feed cats out of one community bowl.

▼ Separate food and water.

▼ If needed, put food on different levels to accommodate the hierarchy.

▼ Wash water bowls daily and replenish with fresh water.

▼ Accommodate individual bowl preferences.

▼ Don't allow moist food to sit out for more than a half hour.

▼ Make mealtime peaceful.

▼ Make sure everyone gets the appropriate amount of food.

▼ Make sure children know not to bother the kitties while they're eating.

▼ If any cat displays a change in appetite, see your veterinarian.

The Litter Box

Litter box problems can occur in any household, regardless of the number of cats, but the chances certainly increase as you add more cats into the mix. I think it's pretty safe to say that if you have several cats, you've probably dealt with a litter box problem or will at some time in the future. Many owners assume the litter box is just the place cats use for elimination—the feline version of a bathroom—and as long as they keep it clean, everyone will be happy. Oh, if only it could be that simple. In reality, a cat's relationship with the litter box is complex and emotional. When more than one cat has to share the box, that relationship can get even more delicate.

OVERCROWDING

You may not want to hear this, but somebody has to tell you—when you have more than one cat, you need more than one litter box. Actually, you should have as many boxes as you have cats. I

CATWISE CAUTION

Any change in litter box habits can be an indication of an
underlying medical problem. There are several conditions that can cause a cat to eliminate away from the box,
and one is lower urinary tract disease. It's not uncommon
for a cat to associate the box itself with the pain he feels
while urinating, and that's why he chooses other locations. Cats with feline lower urinary tract disease
(FLUTD) also have irritated bladders and feel a sense of
urgency even when there's just a drop of urine in the
bladder. You may also notice a cat who goes in and out of
the box frequently, who has a bit of blood mixed in with
his urine, who cries while eliminating, or who is able to
eliminate only small amounts. Other conditions can
cause cats to eliminate outside of the box as well, including diabetes and renal failure. Don't assume that a litter
box problem is behavioral until you've had your cats
checked out by the veterinarian. Urinary problems can be
fatal if the urethra becomes totally blocked, especially for
male cats, who have long narrow urethras. Any change in
a cat's litter box habits or water/food intake should be
brought to the veterinarian's attention immediately.

know you may be shaking your head in disbelief, especially if you
have five or more cats, but if you want to avoid litter box aversion, this is one of those cat rules you shouldn't break. At the
very least, in large multicat homes, get as close as possible to
matching the number of boxes to the cat population. Although

the thought of scooping and scrubbing six or seven boxes may not sound like fun, it's a heck of a lot better than having to replace carpet or refinish floors.

CLEANLINESS

No matter how many cats you have, it's crucial that you keep the litter boxes clean. Nothing will drive a cat away from the box faster than smelly mounds of soiled litter. You should sift and scoop the litter a minimum of twice a day. This is a shock to some of you who may be getting by with peeking at the box only every other day, but trust me, you're headed for trouble. The easiest method is to scoop first thing in the morning and then again before bed. If you really want to avoid potential problems, take a few seconds for an extra litter check when you come home from work. And, of course, if you happen to pass by a litter box in the middle of the day and you notice it has been used, stop to sift and scoop.

Your scooping technique can vary based on the type of litter you use. For scoopable clumping litter, you should have a sturdy slotted shovel. For nonclumping litter, use a slotted shovel to sift through litter for solid waste and a large plastic spoon or non-slotted shovel to scoop out wet mounds of litter. Even with non-clumping litter, the sooner you remove soiled litter, the happier your cats will be.

If you're on a twice-a-day scooping schedule, you can get a plastic garbage bag and make the litter box rounds and then toss the bag in the outside trash. If you want to scoop more often (good for you!), keep a plastic container with a tight-fitting lid near each box. Line the container with a small plastic trash bag or leftover plastic grocery bag. You can lay your shovel on top or get a little container to hold that as well. After you scoop, put the clumps in the container and snap the lid back on. At the end of the day or when the containers start filling up, you can make the rounds to clean them out. If you make it convenient, then you'll be more likely to scoop as often as needed. Of course, if you have ten litter boxes, you may not want ten containers and shovels but at least keep enough strategically placed so you'll have no excuse to shirk your important scooping duties. Scooping more regularly is not only hygienic for your cats and your house, but it may also cut down on tension between cats; some cats won't use the box after another cat has gone there, especially if these two cats are at odds with each other.

The schedule for completely cleaning out the litter and scrubbing the boxes will depend on the type of litter and the habits of your cats. Don't underestimate the importance of scrubbing the box even if you are using scoopable litter. Not all of the urine and feces land exclusively on the litter itself. The sides and bottoms of the boxes will get dirty and need to be scrubbed. Clean the boxes, plastic containers, and shovels with a diluted bleach solution. The diluted bleach will get into all of those microlacerations in the plastic to kill bacteria. Rinse thoroughly with plain water until all traces of the bleach scent are gone. Don't use household cleaners because they're too heavily scented, and definitely don't use ammonia because that'll smell like urine to the cats.

BOX TYPE

COVERED BOXES For many single-cat households this may never be an issue (although I've seen it occur more often than not), but in a multicat environment the use of covered litter boxes is the biggest mistake I see owners make, and it shouldn't be taken lightly. First, let's review why they're no good in general. A covered box traps the odor inside. Owners may love that, but cats hate it. The cover also prevents proper air circulation, so it takes longer for the litter to dry. When it comes to scooping, many owners are less likely to stick to an adequate schedule because of the inconvenience of having to remove the lid. Imagine how unpleasant it must be to step into a dark box filled with damp, smelly litter. Covered boxes also mean twice as much work when it comes time to scrub the boxes.

Those of you who've read *Think Like a Cat* know how I feel about those dreaded covers, but in a multicat home they pose a very real threat: *lack of escape potential*. Humans prefer privacy when it comes to elimination, and we tend to assume that really matters to our cats as well. To a cat, privacy definitely takes a backseat to safety. If cats were really that concerned with privacy, you wouldn't have outdoor kitties eliminating in your front garden. A covered box limits the cat to one entrance/exit. While in the process of elimination, a cat is pretty darn vulnerable, and he certainly doesn't want to get ambushed in there by another cat. In some households, one cat may sit on the lid while another unsuspecting kitty is in the box. The kitty stalker waits for his moment and then pounces just as the victim is exiting the box. It'll take only a couple of these startling encounters for the victim cat to decide to eliminate in a safer location. If all of the litter boxes are covered, that new location may end up being your dining room carpet. Even if your cats aren't feuding, a surprise appearance by a second cat can cause the same reaction. The first cat will avoid the risk of being trapped there again in the future.

Next on my list of negatives about covered boxes has to do with size. The boxes may look large to you, but the actual litter surface isn't any bigger than a regular box. If you're worried about litter scatter or if you have cats who spray inside the box or over the sides, get plastic storage containers and use those as litter boxes. I've found regular litter boxes all to be too small anyway, and my cats have used storage containers for years. The boxes come in all heights, lengths, and widths. This is helpful when you have to have boxes in several locations and not all accommodate a square box. They're also great if you need a couple of extralarge ones in the most frequently used areas.

Many manufacturers make storage containers. Rubbermaid and Sterilite are two popular brands. I particularly like the Sterilite containers because of the simplicity of the square and rectangular shapes, the totally flat bottoms, and the variety of sizes. The plastic of the Sterilite boxes is also exceptionally slick, and so hard litter clumps clean off more easily than they do in a regular litter box or even in the Rubbermaid containers. Sterilite boxes are available at just about any discount store.

To address litter scatter and poorly aimed urination attempts, choose a very high-sided storage container. Cut a U shape on one of the short ends as an easy entrance. The three high sides will contain the litter and urine spray, but the openness of the box will make it convenient for you to scoop. The cats will also have adequate escape potential. And because the Sterilite boxes are a translucent milky color, an approaching cat can see if there's another cat already in the box. Litter will also dry faster than in a covered box. Think of it as a convertible covered box: all the benefits of a covered box without any of the negatives.

SELF-CLEANING BOXES Some owners with large numbers of cats and absolutely no time to scoop may think these boxes are a time-saver, but they can really be a curse. The electronic boxes may deter cats from entering if they approach while the motor and rake are still cleaning up from a previous cat's visit. I also find the actual litter surface areas of the electronic boxes to be too small. The box itself seems large, but that's just because it has to house the motor and the soiled litter receptacle. The rake can also get stuck if the litter clump is exceptionally large. The rake may also get stuck on large clumps of diarrhea as well.

The electronic box deprives the cat owner of a very valuable diagnostic tool—the ability to monitor what is or isn't happening in the litter box. Often the first sign of a potential medical problem is detected by an owner's observation of a change in litter box habits. Noticing an especially hard stool, diarrhea, blood, or mucus, or even parasites in the waste is a valuable red-flag warning. The electronic box prevents you from having that important early warning system.

As for manual self-cleaning boxes—oh boy, are they a waste of time! You'll spend just as much time flipping them over and emptying receptacles as you would if you'd just scoop with a shovel. These boxes also have to be scrubbed, so you'll end up washing the top, the grate, the bottom, and the receptacle. The self-cleaning boxes are also covered, and that adds an extra negative in my book. And as with the electronic box, the actual litter surface size is really quite small in comparison to a regular litter box. In a multicat home, *small* just doesn't cut it.

There are also some very strange self-cleaning boxes that use an automatic whoosh of liquid to clean the permanent substrate so you supposedly never have to change the litter. If the cat happens to be in the box while the cleaning takes place, he ends up with wet paws. Now that's a litter box aversion problem waiting to happen!

LITTER

You may be lucky enough to have a household where all of the cats happily use the same brand of litter. It may even stay that way forever, but in some cases, one or two cats may develop a dislike for the scent, texture, or performance of a particular type or brand.

A basic litter box rule is not to change brands/types of litter abruptly because cats are creatures of habit. You'll be asking for trouble if you suddenly decide to buy the crystallized litter, for example, instead of your usual scoopable variety. When a cat steps into the box, he expects to find the same texture as the last time he visited there.

Perhaps you do want to try a different litter, or maybe you sense one of the cats might be displaying an aversion to the litter—how do you make a change? There are two methods: If you suspect a couple of cats might prefer a different type, you can experiment by setting out an extra box (or more) filled with the new litter. Place the new box near the ones you think are used the most by the discontented cats. You can even set out a few types of litter to give the cats a choice. If you're familiar with the usual litter box routines, you'll be able to tell if that particular cat starts using the new litter. As a creature of habit, a cat tends to use the same technique when positioning himself for elimination and when covering. When a cat has a litter aversion, he may eliminate without digging first or covering afterward. His mission is to get in and out of the box as quickly as possible. Now some cats never dig or cover, but it's important to notice if there's a change in behavior. If a cat who normally scratches at the litter suddenly stops or scratches at the sides of the litter box, the wall behind it, or the floor around it, he may be experiencing a litter aversion. He's attempting to cover but doesn't want to have any more physical contact with the litter than is absolutely necessary. He may also perch on the edge of the box so that his hind legs are propped up on the edge. This results in poor aim, but from the cat's point of view, at least he's *in* the box. A cat may also perch by resting his front paws on the edge. At least the latter position keeps his aim well within the target. A litter aversion can also be the cause if the cat is getting as close to the box as he can but never actually stepping inside. He may eliminate right next to the box or on a nearby mat. It is important to remember that *cats may also stop scratching and covering if the litter is too dirty or if they're experiencing a medical problem.*

It's not uncommon in big feline families to have one or two cats who prefer a specific type of litter. You may need to keep a few of the boxes filled with that preference. You won't be able to stop other cats from using it, but at least your picky kitty will be happy. If you find that the box or boxes containing that litter start getting heavily used, it's probably a sign that most of the cats prefer it and it's time to switch litter types in more of the boxes. Cats are very tactile, and the texture of a litter is important. With multiple cats you have to be prepared that not all will share the same preferences.

If you're having trouble scooping the litter because urine clumps are breaking apart and crumbling, switch to a multicat-formula litter. Also, you may need to refresh the litter with a top-up. Multicat-formula litters form harder clumps that withstand heavier traffic and can make a big difference in keeping the litter box clean.

The gradual changeover is another method of changing litter brands or types. You add a small amount of the new litter into the current brand. Every few days you can gradually increase the proportion of new to old. If you begin to notice the start of litter box rejection, or if you see less covering of waste than normal, it means you're moving too quickly. Slow down; if you still notice a problem, it may indicate that the type of litter you chose will not be acceptable to the majority of the cats.

Keep in mind that when switching to a different type of litter, such as going from clay to scoopable or from scoopable to crystallized, the performance of the litter will not be optimal because of the noncompatible formulations. Scoopable litter may not clump effectively while there is still a large amount of regular clay litter in the box. Hang in there during the transition because the litter performance will improve as the proportions change.

When adding a new cat into the current household, if he has been accustomed to a particular type of litter, use that in his sanctuary room until he gets his bearings. You can then do a gradual changeover. If you aren't sure which type of litter the cat would prefer, or if you're rescuing a stray cat, it's usually best to start with unscented scoopable litter since an outdoor cat would have been used to eliminating in sand and soil. If you normally use a very specialized litter in your home, set out two boxes in the sanctuary room so the new cat has a choice. He may go right away for the specialized kind, or you can do a gradual change-over once he has settled in.

A litter aversion can occur for reasons you might never think of, even if you're using the same brand of litter you always have. If you recently started adding commercial litter additives, the scent or texture changes may be unpleasant to some of the cats if too much is added to the box.

If you use plastic liners, one of your cats may dislike the sound or feel of them. Many cats dislike the way their claws can get hung up in the plastic as they try to scratch the litter. Liners are a bad idea anyway. They don't fit right and often create pockets where urine can puddle and remain unabsorbed. I once had a client who was using kitchen trash bags as liners. She went to a lot of trouble to ensure the bags fit properly in the litter boxes, even going so far as to tape the edges down. Her cats didn't seem to mind them; then suddenly two of the four cats stopped using the litter boxes at the same time. When I was called in, I discovered after much questioning that the owner had recently started buying lemon-scented garbage bags. Cats don't like the scent of citrus, so imagine how displeased they were with the condition of their litter boxes.

Sometimes, if one of the cats in the home is ill, another cat may be afraid to use the same box if he detects an odor from the sick cat.

LITTER LEVELS When you go from one cat to two or more, your days of buying small, easy-to-carry boxes or bags of litter are over. You have probably now entered into the world of the warehouse club shopper or at least learned which stores carry the super-duper jumbo-sized containers of litter. There are two things a cat owner never wants to run out of: food and litter.

The second half of establishing a good scooping/sifting schedule is maintaining a consistent litter level. Depending upon how much a particular box gets used, you'll have to top off the remaining litter with a fresh supply. In general, you'll probably have to do this every couple of days. One thing I often see on house calls is an insufficient amount of litter in the boxes. Although you have five or six boxes to maintain, this isn't the time to skimp on litter levels. There should always be enough clean litter in the box for at least three visits. If some of your cats are very enthusiastic litter scratchers, ensure that there's a little extra in the boxes they tend to frequent. When you go to check the box, you don't want to see a pile of litter on one side and the bottom of the box on the other. This can set you up for a litter box aversion problem. Even if some of your cats don't mind the low litter level, it'll mean a smelly box as the urine just sits unabsorbed in the box. On the other hand, don't fill the box to the brim with litter because that's a waste. It makes it harder to scoop, there's more of a chance of litter scatter, and some cats may object to having to perch on mountains of litter.

BOX LOCATIONS There is an unbreakable rule of litter box placement that most experienced cat owners already know: *Never locate the box near the food and water.* If you didn't know that and you've broken this rule, I'll bet you're in the middle of a litter box aversion problem right now. Why is that an unbreakable rule? Cats don't eat where they eliminate. On the most basic level that makes common sense. Humans don't tend to eat in the bathroom either, but for a cat this behavior is rooted in survival. The cat eliminates away from the nest, so he won't attract predators with the scent of his waste. Even the most pampered indoor cat shares this instinct. If the food bowl in your home is near the litter box, move it right now. If a litter box must be kept in the same room as the food bowl (as in the case of a new cat's sanctuary room), it should be placed on the wall opposite the food. Also, make sure the box is not too close to appliances that might startle a cat. The sudden sound of a washing machine could be a real deterrent.

TERRITORIAL CONSIDERATIONS With multiple cats you not only need multiple litter boxes, you need multiple litter box locations. You may think you're being efficient by creating a "litter box room," but you run the risk of an aversion problem. Why can't you just place ten boxes side by side in one room and make that the official feline bathroom? As you may remember from chapters 1 and 3, everything in your home is part of overlapping home ranges and territories. One of the cats may have claimed the area near the laundry room, and if you've placed all of the litter boxes there, one or more of the lower-ranking cats may be reluctant to enter. You can probably tell who tends to dominate certain areas. When considering litter box placement, scatter them throughout the home to cover all bases. If one or two of the cats are especially timid or low ranking, don't ask them to cross into a higher-ranking cat's turf in order to gain access to the box.

I have three cats who have clearly carved out individual home ranges and territories within my home, although they all share one another's turf without a problem. I've set up a litter box in each cat's territory and even though they all use each of the boxes, I notice that they use the box within their own area most often. I believe much of the reason there has never been a litter box problem among my cats is because I addressed that territorial issue immediately to make sure there would be no reason for any of them ever to feel worried.

ESCAPE POTENTIAL As I mentioned while discussing covered boxes, privacy is important to our bathroom behavior, and we mistakenly believe we need to provide an abundance of that for our cats as well. Yes, a certain degree of privacy is needed; after all, very few cats want the litter box right in the middle of the family room where the children are noisily playing video games, but some owners go to extremes to create privacy. Much of the privacy owners create is primarily for *their* benefit and not the cats'. Although many owners simply don't want litter boxes in the main living areas, too much privacy can be to a cat's detriment.

A cat is extremely vulnerable when in the litter box. It's a time when a higher-ranking cat may choose to ambush a lower-ranking one. A cat caught eliminating in a box that is "claimed" by another cat may find himself backed into a corner before he can finish urinating. The need for escape potential isn't even limited to feline confrontations: dogs and young children can also be a threat. When a cat is taking care of his litter box business, that's not the time he should have to worry about defending himself.

There are two steps to creating optimal escape. The first involves creating an open box so the cat has as many ways to leap out in a hurry as possible. This way, if a perceived threat approaches from any direction, the cat in the box can go the opposite way. Even if you have uncovered boxes, but they're hidden in closets or wedged in corners, you've reduced the cat's escape potential by half. The solution is as simple as keeping the box in the open and sliding it out several inches from the wall. Often that can be enough for the cats to feel they can dart out the back or side if necessary.

The second aspect of creating escape potential involves providing adequate *warning time*. When a cat is in the box, the more visual advantage he has to see if someone is approaching, the better. If you're experiencing a tension-related elimination problem, there's a good chance the soiled areas are in open, "escapable" areas. The frightened cat doesn't want to be caught off guard in the litter box, so he may choose the dining room, where there are usually two entrances. The cat may eliminate on the carpet at the wall opposite a door. This way, he has the most visual warning to see who might be coming. Lower-ranking cats may also choose rooms that aren't officially "claimed" or ones that aren't used often by owners. That's another reason why dining rooms seem to be a popular choice. Not only do most dining rooms have two entrances, but for many families they are used only when entertaining company. Guest rooms are another popular choice. The cat associates these places with neutral territory or the perimeter of the nest. Some cats may choose the owner's master bedroom because they think of that as a safe haven. Those cats need escape potential but also are comforted by your familiar scent, which is concentrated in that room.

Place litter boxes in areas of rooms that allow the cats to see the doorway. If a cat can see down the hallway as well, even bet-

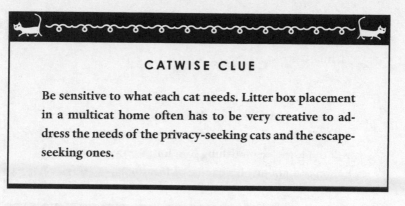

CATWISE CLUE

Be sensitive to what each cat needs. Litter box placement in a multicat home often has to be very creative to address the needs of the privacy-seeking cats and the escape-seeking ones.

ter. Create as much of a visual advantage as possible while still maintaining enough privacy to satisfy you and your cats. For some households where the tension is extremely high, the need for escape should take precedence over any need for privacy. In those situations, if the box has to be in the middle of the room to create security, then that's where it'll have to be (temporarily, don't worry). If you place the boxes in areas that create security, it can mean the difference between cautious reaction and over-reaction with claws.

Consider escape potential before deciding to put a litter box in the basement with a cat flap in the basement door. I've even seen owners put cat flaps on laundry room doors. The cat flap means one cat still faces the risk of suddenly encountering another cat without warning at very close range.

SPRAYING

Urine-marking is a behavior displayed by both confident and less-confident cats. It's not just "turf marking," but rather a complex form of feline communication, a language all its own. It can be a sexual announcement, a territorial marker, a display of aggres-

CATWISE CAUTION

Never, never, never rub a cat's nose in his urine or feces!
This is inhumane, extremely stressful, and confusing for
the cat, and will only backfire on your training. The cat
will think you're punishing him for the very act of elimination and not just his choice of location.

sion, a response to another cat's threat, a victory display after an
aggressive confrontation, or a display of uncertainty. It's important to realize that where cats roam freely, spraying is a normal
aspect of feline life. It's a vital aspect of their social structure. I
want to impress on you that it's not a so-called "bad" behavior.
The sprayer is not being deliberately bad or spiteful. When a cat
sprays, he is reacting to a specific situation in a typically feline
way. That said, it doesn't make it a good thing when it's happening in your home.

Spraying is different than indiscriminate urination, and it's important for an owner to be able to differentiate between the two.
Indiscriminate urination mostly happens on horizontal surfaces
and is commonly associated with litter box rejection or urinary
tract problems. It can be due to a social problem in the feline
household if one cat feels too afraid to approach the litter box, as
described previously in this chapter.

Spraying, on the other hand, is usually performed against vertical objects and is used for purposes of communication and
marking. The cat remains standing, as opposed to the normal
squatting posture for urination. He backs up to the object, his tail

begins to quiver, and he often kneads the ground with his front feet. He may even half close his eyes and break into what looks like a silly grin. Soon, a spray of urine is sent vertically out toward the targeted object. By standing, the cat is able to aim for nose height. This way, a passing cat surely won't miss it.

Spraying can also be performed on horizontal objects such as carpets, beds, couches, or tables. Your clue is that the urine will often be in a thin stream as opposed to a puddle. Sometimes, spraying is mistaken for indiscriminate urination because, for instance, the owner notices only the urine puddle on the carpet by the wall and isn't aware that it dripped from the vertical target. (There is also a behavior known as horizontal nonspray marking, which is covered in the next section.)

A higher-ranking cat often sprays in more than one area to make sure other felines in the home understand the wide reach of this top cat's domain. A dominant cat entering a new turf may spray as an announcement of his arrival or as a warning so another cat doesn't get any ideas. An outdoor cat will usually routinely spray as he goes around the perimeter of his territory.

A lower-ranking cat tends to limit his spraying to one or two areas, often in an attempt to carve out a little territory for himself, gather information (as a response to a direct threat from another cat), or as a passive display of aggression. If a less-confident cat is confronted with a direct threat, he may feel more comfortable spraying after the opponent has left because he knows the other cat is too strong or dominant to provoke. In this case, spraying becomes his response to a threat without risking an actual confrontation and potential injury. With ongoing disputes in the environment, lower-ranking males may engage in a "spraying war" instead of a face-to-face confrontation.

Although most people associate spraying behavior with male

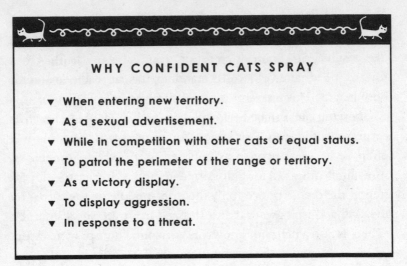

WHY CONFIDENT CATS SPRAY

▼ When entering new territory.

▼ As a sexual advertisement.

▼ While in competition with other cats of equal status.

▼ To patrol the perimeter of the range or territory.

▼ As a victory display.

▼ To display aggression.

▼ In response to a threat.

cats, females may also spray when threatened. In free-roaming environments, it's normal for females to spray when entering a hunting ground.

Sometimes a cat will exhibit a spraying posture without actually spraying urine. A less-confident cat may display this because

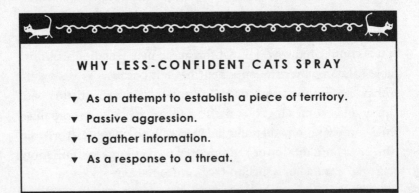

WHY LESS-CONFIDENT CATS SPRAY

▼ As an attempt to establish a piece of territory.

▼ Passive aggression.

▼ To gather information.

▼ As a response to a threat.

he's too nervous to risk the response. It's almost as if he knows he won't be able to back up his threat.

Spraying by a less-confident cat is often used to gather very valuable information. This is especially the case when a new cat enters the environment. The new cat's response to the spray-marking cat gives the "sprayer" information he doesn't have the nerve to gather through a direct encounter. He will later return to his spray-marked area to see if there was a response to his communication.

HORIZONTAL NONSPRAY MARKING

Yes, it exists. Just when you thought you were getting this all figured out! Confident and less-confident cats may engage in this behavior, which involves squatting and depositing urine and feces. Depositing feces in this way is known as *middening*. In free-roaming situations, a confident cat may leave feces as an olfactory and visual marker on the boundaries of his territory, in the middle of a challenged path, or where he thinks a rival may come along. This usually occurs in addition to a round of urine spray-marking on trees and bushes. Less-confident cats may also do this to claim particular areas, because they may be too intimidated to engage in spray-marking, a direct threat. Leaving urine in a horizontal place appears less challenging to the other cats.

It's often very difficult to differentiate horizontal nonspray marking from indiscriminate urination or litter box aversion. You should first run down your checklist to rule out medical conditions, litter aversion, location aversion, need for more litter boxes, need for escape, and so forth. If you've satisfactorily addressed all of those, then you might be dealing with horizontal nonspray-marking behavior. This then becomes a social issue, and you have to look at the relationships between the cats and

how territory is being divided and handled. To treat this problem, follow the instructions below.

TREATMENT FOR SPRAYING

Before I run through some techniques for dealing with a spraying
problem, you have to try to figure out the cause. Cats don't just
spray without a reason, so you must examine the social environment within your cat community. Its time to play detective.

Where is your cat (or cats) spraying? Under what circumstances? Is it in one area? Perhaps a lower-ranking cat is trying to
establish a little piece of his own territory. Did you bring a new
cat into the home? Every time you add or subtract a cat it shakes
up the hierarchy. One of your resident cats may be trying to see
how dominant this new cat is. Observe the overall behavior of
your cats. Do you notice any changes recently? If you know
which cat is doing the spraying, try to remember what happened
just minutes before. Perhaps one cat always seems to spray after
a confrontation with another particular cat. Is there a pattern?

Look at the targeted locations for clues as well. There are
claimed territories and neutral pathways within your home. If
you really know your cats (and they're creatures of habit, so it
gets easier as time goes on), you might be able to tell if perhaps
the spraying occurs along a pathway—perhaps warning other
cats not to enter a claimed territory. Maybe a neutral pathway is
being sprayed because there just isn't enough territory, and a
lower-ranking cat is trying to establish some turf.

If the target areas are under windows or on a wall opposite a
window that looks out onto an active yard, the problem could
simply be that a cat has noticed an unfamiliar cat on the property.
That happens in single-cat households very often, but in a multicat home it can occur because the sprayer knows there just isn't

any more territory to divide up. If you allow some or all of your cats outdoors, one may spray after returning indoors if he comes across a cat outside. A kitty's adventures outdoors can create insecurity because a cat may pick up the scent of another cat while outside or maybe even engage in an actual confrontation. Once back indoors, he may reinforce his territory and reassure himself by spraying within the safety of his own home.

Don't restrict yourself to thinking the spraying is either the top-ranking cat asserting himself or the lowest-ranking cat trying to establish some tiny piece of territory. In my house calls, I've found that the middle cats are often the ones who squabble. The top cat may clearly know he's the head honcho, and the lowest cat may have long ago settled onto the bottom rung. Those middle cats, however, can be discontented with their positions in the hierarchy. Sometimes it's the cat you least expected because spraying can seem very secretive to humans. You have to look at your home from a cat's point of view.

It's hard to treat a spraying problem in a multicat environment if you don't know who the culprit is. Some cats are very open about their displays, but many engage in covert behavior. If you have no idea which cat is spraying, you can ask your veterinarian for some fluorescein capsules. This harmless ophthalmic dye is placed in capsules and then given to a cat orally. You then purchase a black light. Nature's Miracle makes an excellent one. The black light will cause all of the urine marks to fluoresce, but the fluorescein-stained urine will *really* stand out. To use the black light, darken the room before turning on the light. Hold the light a few inches away from the carpet or other objects in the room. Give the fluorescein capsule to the most likely suspect. After a few days, if you don't see any traces, you can move on to the next likely suspect.

If there are just a few specific areas where the spraying is being done, you can set up a video camera. The inexpensive video baby monitors that are available make this very simple. The monitors can be hooked up to record to your VCR, so you won't have to camp out at the monitor twenty-four hours a day waiting to catch someone in the act.

SEEK AND DESTROY While some sprayed areas may be obvious to the eye and definitely to the nose, others may not. Some cats pick the most unlikely places, and you have to find all of the soiled spots. Use the black light to identify all areas that'll need to be cleaned. You can either clean each area as you go, if there aren't too many soiled spots, or you can mark the areas for easy identification later. When I'm dealing with multiple areas in a client's home, I outline the soiled areas with painter's tape. The bright color is easy to see so you won't overlook any marked spots, and it's easy to remove. When you're doing your identification process, be sure to mark soiled walls, floor, carpets, and furniture. A cat may have gotten onto a piece of furniture and marked the wall behind it. Check closets, under beds, and behind doors. Some cats spray shoes and clothing, so run the black light over everything in the bottom of your closets as well as the lower portions of hanging clothes. It's also important to use the black light at the litter box areas in case one or more of the cats are spraying around the box itself, the room entrance, or the walls nearby.

A note about the black light: Be prepared when you first turn it on and start viewing the room. Things may look much worse than you ever imagined. The black light illuminates every urine drop, but it also will illuminate spots where cats have vomited or had diarrhea accidents, so don't panic when you shine the light across the carpet and everything looks polka-dotted. In a multicat home where hairballs are a way of life, you're bound to see many illuminated spots that aren't urine stains. If you're in doubt, clean those areas anyway or be brave and get down on the carpet and stick your nose right over the spot. It may not be one of the more glamorous aspects of being a cat owner, but if you're going to solve the problem, you have to be a relentless detective.

CLEAN STAINS AND NEUTRALIZE ODORS Even as you're trying to figure out the cause of the behavior, you have to clean the soiled areas to prevent repeat visits or a trigger for other cats to start spraying in the same locations.

If the soiled area is on the floor, cleanup is much easier because you can simply wipe up the urine and then treat the spot with the odor neutralizer. If you're cleaning carpet, use paper towels to first absorb as much liquid as you can. Then use an enzymatic pet stain remover/odor neutralizer. Nature's Miracle is one of the most popular brands, but there are others out there as well. Just make sure it contains enzymes because that's the only way to neutralize the odor. Regular carpet or household cleaners will only mask the odor, and the residual odor molecules be detected by a cat's sensitive nose. To use the odor neutralizer, spray or pour it over the soiled carpet.

Once you've applied the odor neutralizer to the carpet, gently agitate the carpet fibers with your fingers. Don't rub the carpet with a towel. Let the neutralizer sit for several minutes, and then use towels to blot up the moisture. In some cases, where urine may have gone through the carpet and into the padding, reapply more neutralizer and let it sit according to the manufacturer's directions. Then again, blot up the moisture with towels. To get up as much moisture as possible, place a heavy object over the towel and leave it in place for a while. Replace with fresh towels as needed. After you've removed as much moisture as possible, place a small fan over the area if it still feels damp, or if you have to treat the padding as well.

If the soiled area has been repeatedly urine-sprayed, you may need to wet it first. A heavy buildup of old urine can sometimes overpower the enzymes. Use plain water first to moisten the carpet and then blot. You can then use the enzymatic neutralizer as you would for a fresh spray mark.

Enzymatic odor neutralizers are available at pet supply stores. They also work well for other stains such as vomit, blood, and diarrhea. In my home, we never let the supply of enzymatic neutralizer run out.

Don't use the odor neutralizer on vertical targets such as the wall or table legs. For those areas you're going to use plain water (yes, you read right), then you'll use another product specifically for those spots. I'll explain that in the next segment.

CHANGE THE CAT'S ASSOCIATION WITH THE AREA Cats are creatures of habit, and even if you've discovered and destroyed the spray marks, mere habit can drive cats back to those areas again and again. Fortunately, you can break the behavior pattern.

In the last section on spraying, I told you not to use the stain and odor neutralizer on the vertical areas. The reason is a product called Feliway, which was originally designed to help correct feline spray-marking. Feliway contains synthetic feline facial pheromones. Pheromones are scent chemicals that cats release from various scent glands on their bodies. When a cat urine-marks, he's releasing scent chemicals, along with his urine, that are released only when the cat is in a state of excitation. There are also scent glands on the cat's face, and you've probably seen your cat facially rub objects in the home or even on you. The facial pheromones are released when a cat is in a calm state, and they have a calming effect on cats when they smell them later. The synthetic pheromones in Feliway have that same effect. Each cat interprets the synthetic pheromones as his own. This helps correct spraying problems because it can aid in changing the cat's association with an area, and cats don't urine-mark where they facially rub.

After you have cleaned them with water, spray Feliway over the vertical areas where your cat has urine-marked. It will help shift his mind-set when he approaches that spot. If he thinks he facially rubbed there, he'll start to assume it's a more secure and comforting area rather than a threatening area. The reason you should clean those soiled vertical areas only with water is because enzymatic neutralizers may inactivate the pheromones in Feliway.

Feliway is available at pet supply stores, veterinary clinics, and online, and it comes in two forms—a spray and Feliway Comfort Zone, an electric plug-in diffuser. Depending on your specific circumstances, one might be better than the other. If there are multiple urine-sprayed areas, or if the spots are in hidden places, you should use the spray bottle. Spray each urine-marked area once every twelve hours for the first month to maintain a consistent pheromone level. Hold the bottle four inches away from the object and eight inches up from the ground. The eight-inch height puts the pheromones right at nose height for the average cat. Feliway should be sprayed about a half hour before bringing the cats back into the area. Once the spray dries, you won't be able to detect any scent, but your cats will discover the positive pheromones.

Don't limit the use of Feliway to those specific areas. Spray prominent objects in the room (again, eight inches up from the ground) so the cats come across them as they walk through the area. This can be helpful if a cat walks into a room with the intention of spraying. If he is in an agitated or anxious state, those calming pheromones may help him feel more relaxed and secure.

The plug-in diffusers are especially useful if the spray-marked area is limited to one room, but you may want to place one in each "insecure" room. Use the diffuser in the areas where your cats tend to spend the most time to help keep tension on a lower level. The diffuser can also make your life much easier because you don't have to remember to spray twice a day.

If you use the bottled version, after the first month of twice-a-day applications, you can cut back to once daily for the next month if things have improved. If not, continue the twice-a-day schedule a month longer. After a successful month of spraying once a day, maintain a schedule of several applications a week.

Feliway has many other uses beyond litter box problems. You can use it in a sanctuary room when bringing in a new cat, when moving to a new home to help the cats adjust more quickly, or during tense periods in your home. Basically, whenever a calm environment is needed, this product can help.

INTERACTIVE PLAY THERAPY The next way to change the spraying cat's association with the area is to conduct play sessions with him near those targeted spots. One of the best ways to improve a cat's mind-set is to trigger his prey drive. You'll use the interactive play session in two ways. First, conduct individual sessions a couple of times a day in those areas. You will have to separate the cats, so if more than one cat is spraying, do separate sessions for each one. If there are several urine-sprayed areas, rotate your sessions to cover each one fairly regularly. These sessions will help the cat think of these previously insecure areas as safe and positive and will put the cat in a more confident state of mind. It takes confidence to shift into prey drive and be a predator.

The second way you'll use interactive play therapy is to distract a cat from a potential spray target. When using this technique, it's important to get to the cat *before* he actually engages in the spraying behavior. You won't be able to distract him once he begins spraying. While your immediate reaction might be to want to yell at him or chase him away, that is actually counterproductive. If you yell or chase (or worse, hit or throw some-

thing at him), you'll only prevent him from spraying in that particular area at that particular time or from spraying in your presence. He'll likely become a more secretive sprayer; your yelling
at him doesn't alleviate his need to urine-mark. It also damages
the emotional bond between the two of you. Instead, use a positive form of distraction to change his mind-set immediately.
Keep a stash of toys hidden in various places, and when you suspect a potential spraying, distract the cat by tossing a toy gently
to get his attention. You can use any type of toy you know he
likes. If you're in the midst of a spraying crisis, you might want
to keep a couple of toys in your pocket. You can also use an interactive toy. The Dragonfly and Cat Dancer are great for emergency distraction because they can be curled up for easy storage
and stashed around the house.

If you know a toy won't distract him or he has started spraying, you can use something to startle him mildly, such as a shake
can (an empty soda can with a few pennies inside). If you're in
the kitchen, make a noise with a pot. But don't let him see you or
he'll soon learn to be more covert. When using shake cans, water
sprayers, or any other kind of behavior interruption, never let
the cat see you because it can create fear. If the cat associates the
sound or the squirt with that particular area and thinks of it in
terms of an "act of God," he's more likely to make the connection that the area isn't a place he wants to be. Use the minimal
amount of startle-stimulus necessary.

When you see your little sprayer successfully using the litter
box, praise him afterward, especially if he had been about to spray
in an inappropriate place and was successfully redirected to the box.

STRATEGICALLY PLACED FOOD BOWLS This is an old standby
counterconditioning technique often used when trying to correct
a feline inappropriate elimination problem of any kind. Cats don't

eliminate where they eat, so if you place a few extra little food bowls (containing dry food) at targeted spray areas, it may help change the cat's association. In some cases I've seen cats who will spray at the area anyway, but it's a method that does have its merits. I think this is more successful in combination with Feliway and interactive playtime. If you do choose to try this, you should maintain the normal feeding stations and be sure to apportion the cat's regular servings so you are not overfeeding.

DETERRENTS AND PROTECTION If there are targeted areas where you simply can't do the playtime or place the food bowls (hopefully you can still use Feliway), you can set up temporary deterrents to protect further damage. Cover the areas with a piece of plastic carpet runner. You can then spray Feliway on the plastic. If it's an area where you don't want your cat at all, set up the plastic carpet runner with some shake cans out in front to prevent your cat from getting there. He won't like the shake cans, and they also serve as an audible warning system for you. You can also place strips of Sticky Paws on the carpet in front of the area. I don't like to use deterrent methods because they still leave the cat in a negative mind-set, but these will at least keep difficult areas from sustaining any more damage. You still need to do all of the positive behavior modification work, though. Even if you can't specifically play with the cat in that area, you should still do regular play sessions with him, use Feliway, and continue to seek out the original cause of his anxiety.

CHANGE THE CATS' ASSOCIATIONS WITH ONE ANOTHER Changing a cat's impression with soiled areas is only part of the job. You also have to help spraying cats and their opponents come to a peaceful understanding. If you make only environmental changes, the cats' opinions of one another may still remain hostile or tense.

Make sure you've made those necessary environmental changes such as ensuring each cat has adequate territory and evaluating your litter box setups. Then it's time to work on relationships with a more intense form of the diversion technique. When cats are interacting, watch for specific body postures and use an interactive toy to redirect the aggressive cat's behavior. This is important in order to break any ongoing behavior patterns cats may have established. Diversion techniques are very effective and are mapped out in detail in chapter 5.

If the relationship between the spraying cat and one or more of the others is continually tense or even overtly hostile, they may need a total reintroduction. Sometimes the best way to correct the situation is to start from scratch and gradually expose them to one another under positive circumstances. If spraying behavior is caused by the addition of a new cat, keep the newcomer in a sanctuary room and slow down the introduction.

INDISCRIMINATE URINATION

If the cat is not spray-marking, then you're dealing with indiscriminate urination. As mentioned in the beginning of this chapter, there are many possible causes. You must rule out medical possibilities first, most prominently urinary tract infection.

After your cat gets a clean bill of health, go down your checklist to see if it's a litter aversion, location aversion, too-dirty box, overcrowding, and so forth. Get out your black light and find those soiled areas. If a cat repeatedly soils in a particular area, place a litter box there temporarily. He's letting you know his location preference, and it'll ease his tension tremendously if you

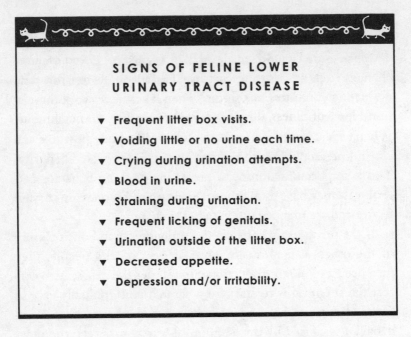

SIGNS OF FELINE LOWER URINARY TRACT DISEASE

▼ Frequent litter box visits.

▼ Voiding little or no urine each time.

▼ Crying during urination attempts.

▼ Blood in urine.

▼ Straining during urination.

▼ Frequent licking of genitals.

▼ Urination outside of the litter box.

▼ Decreased appetite.

▼ Depression and/or irritability.

just provide him with what he needs. Keep the box in that spot and when he starts to use it routinely and no longer soils the carpet, you can gradually move it to a more convenient location if necessary. If you do relocate the box, move it *a couple of feet a day.* I'm not kidding. An abrupt change in the location will send him right back to urinating on your carpet. If you move it a little a day, he won't notice. The final location you select must meet his needs as well as his original spot. If he absolutely refuses to eliminate anywhere but that location, even after behavior modification and the resolution of any social issues, his chosen location may be the only area where he feels safe.

Sometimes a cat forms a negative association with the box during an illness, urinary tract infection, or a time when he experienced discomfort from diarrhea or constipation. It doesn't have to be a long-term illness or discomfort for him to connect the box with the pain he feels. A short bout of painful, cramping diarrhea can do it. If the problem doesn't resolve itself when the cat gets better, set out a totally new box with a different brand of litter near but not too close to his original box. If you're not sure which is his favorite, set out a few boxes in various locations. In some cases of illness, discomfort, or injury, the cat's negative as-

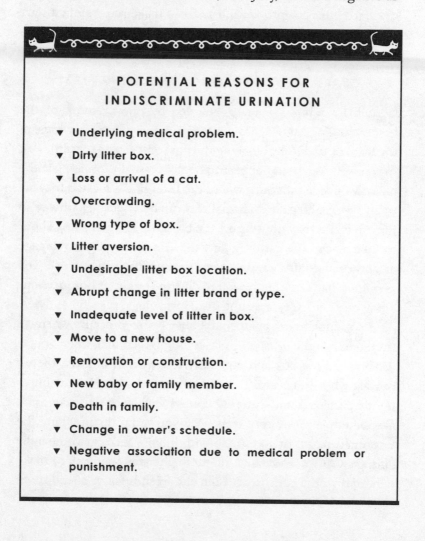

POTENTIAL REASONS FOR INDISCRIMINATE URINATION

▼ Underlying medical problem.

▼ Dirty litter box.

▼ Loss or arrival of a cat.

▼ Overcrowding.

▼ Wrong type of box.

▼ Litter aversion.

▼ Undesirable litter box location.

▼ Abrupt change in litter brand or type.

▼ Inadequate level of litter in box.

▼ Move to a new house.

▼ Renovation or construction.

▼ New baby or family member.

▼ Death in family.

▼ Change in owner's schedule.

▼ Negative association due to medical problem or punishment.

sociation may also include difficulty getting in and out of the box. If you think that's the case, set up some large but low-sided boxes in the areas where he tends to eliminate.

The treatment for indiscriminate urination starts with uncovering the cause and then thoroughly cleaning and neutralizing the soiled areas as described above. Look over the list of potential causes of litter box problems listed, but make sure you first start at the veterinary clinic to rule out underlying medical causes.

GUARDING, PATROLLING, AND BEING FIRST

Certain litter boxes may be guarded by one or more of the higher-ranking cats. Guarding behavior can be very obvious, in the form of physically blocking the box, or it can be so subtle you may miss it. What may appear to be a cat casually lounging in the hallway outside the room where the litter box is located may actually be a cat on guard. The hallway can be a neutral pathway, so the other cats may not suspect the blocking or ambushing about to take place. The cat on guard may not even need to engage in an actual confrontation—mere intimidation may work well enough. That's another reason to ensure your litter box locations allow easy access, escape, and visual warning.

A common and very normal behavior often occurs when it's time to scrub the litter box. Have you noticed that when you've just washed the box and replenished it with fresh litter, there's one cat who always insists on being first to use it? He may impatiently pace back and forth as he waits for you to finish. In some cases, he might not even wait until you've finished refilling the box, or he might sit and watch with intense focus as you handle "his" box. It's not unusual for the higher-ranking cats to make sure they're the ones to christen the fresh litter or spend more time in the litter box. This is normal behavior.

Scratching Behavior

It's imperative that a cat owner understand scratching behavior and how to supply what a cat needs. Failure to do both usually results not only in damage to the furniture but in damage to the relationship. Tragically, an owner's lack of understanding of normal scratching needs often leads to the unnecessary and inhumane act of declawing.

SCRATCHING BASICS

Many people believe a cat scratches just to sharpen her claws. While scratching is an innate behavior and provides the opportunity to remove the outer dead sheaths from the nail, that's only a very minor part of the story.

MARKING As you've read, a cat is a master at communication and makes use of every form of communication available to keep things running smoothly in and around her turf. When a cat scratches an object, the claw marks serve as a visual marker. Since cats keep the peace through avoidance and respecting distance, this sign is very helpful. An approaching cat can see the mark from a distance and perhaps avoid trouble by realizing she's in someone else's territory. There are also scent glands in the cat's paw pads, so when she presses her paws against whatever she is scratching, she leaves a scent. Even cats who are declawed may still exhibit a form of scratching behavior in order to leave olfactory marks on objects.

EMOTIONS AND DISPLACEMENT Scratching is one way a cat may display emotion, such as excitement when you walk in the door at the end of the day. She may run over to the scratching post when she hears your key in the lock. In anticipation of dinner, she may also scratch when she sees you heading toward the kitchen.

She may also take out her social frustrations or other stresses on the post. Displacement may be exhibited by grooming or through scratching. If a cat is denied access to something she wants, she may relieve her frustration by engaging in a healthy scratching session at the nearest post.

STRETCHING AND TONING Last but not least is the incredible stretch that a good scratch provides. A cat has a very flexible spine, and she can curl up into the tightest ball during naps. Imagine how incredibly good it must feel to sink her claws into the top of the scratching post and stretch her back and shoulder muscles. It's not at all unusual to see a cat head for the scratching post immediately after napping or after a long session of windowsill bird-watching. Of my three cats, my twenty-year-old kitty, Albie, sleeps the entire night on the bed with me. When my alarm goes off in the morning, as I'm reaching over to turn it off, I can hear

Albie vigorously scratching at the post near the bed. Those twenty-year-old muscles really appreciate being able to unkink so effectively. Albie needs that stretch so much that even if he gets up in the middle of the night to go to the litter box, he'll stop at the scratching post first.

TYPES OF POSTS

Cats can scratch vertically and horizontally. Most tend to scratch on vertical objects because it leaves a more easily seen visual mark, and it better enables them to get a good stretch. However, some cats prefer horizontal scratching and many kitties enjoy both.

The best type of vertical post to look for is tall, sturdy, and covered in a rough material such as sisal. Carpet-covered posts commonly found in pet supply stores are a waste of money. When a cat sinks her nails into the post, she wants the right kind of resistance to pull off those dead nail sheaths. With a carpet-covered post, a cat just tends to get her nails caught up in the fiber loops. Don't waste your money. Your cats don't care about brightly covered carpets or toys dangling from a spring on the top. If your cats are scratching the furniture, then you bought the wrong posts.

You can find sisal-covered posts in many pet supply stores, but don't just settle for any sisal-covered one. The post should also be tall and sturdy, with a good heavy base. If the post wobbles, it's unacceptable. It also needs to be tall enough for a cat to get a full stretch. In addition to sisal, you can find rope-wrapped posts. They're good as well, but you may have to periodically tighten the rope.

If you're handy, you may want to construct some scratching posts for your cats. You can wrap them with sisal, rope, or carpet as long as the *backside* faces out. It may not look very attractive, but it's a great use for carpet scraps. If you already have a scratching post that isn't getting any use, you can rewrap it with a more appealing material. Some cats like to scratch on bare wood. If you're uncertain about what kind of posts to buy, look at the areas where your cats are currently scratching to get an idea of their texture preferences.

I've come across a never-fail sisal-covered post that cats love. It's made by TopCat Products (see Appendix). The post itself is round, and my cats just love wrapping their paws around it. It's also tall and sturdy. The TopCat posts in my home have taken much abuse from my enthusiastic cats, and they hold up beautifully. They also make one that has a sisal-covered base for combination vertical/horizontal scratching. The post comes treated with catnip inside, so it'll most likely be a big hit right out of the box.

For horizontal scratching pads, you can find sisal-covered scratching pads and corrugated cardboard pads at just about every pet supply store. Cats also love corrugated cardboard. There are corrugated scratching ramps, so you can meet any scratching position preference. If you choose the corrugated cardboard pads or ramps, look for wide ones. The Cosmic Catnip Alpine Scratcher is a terrific option.

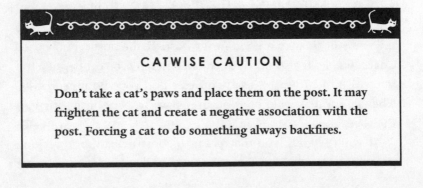

CATWISE CAUTION

Don't take a cat's paws and place them on the post. It may frighten the cat and create a negative association with the post. Forcing a cat to do something always backfires.

Cats generally take to the right kind of scratching post immediately, but if you think your cats aren't, use an interactive toy and play around the post to get their interest. Once they sink their claws in, they'll be convinced. If you've ever punished your cats for scratching on inappropriate objects, you may have to entice them a little because they might be afraid to scratch in your presence.

SO MANY CATS, TOO FEW POSTS

Since scratching is a marking behavior, a couple of your cats may not enjoy having to share a post, and each cat may have different needs in terms of when, where, and how they like to scratch. You may encounter territorial and hierarchical issues, so one or two posts won't be sufficient; in a multicat home you need multiple posts—including some horizontal scratching pads. One good thing is if you have at least one cat tree and your cats scratch the support posts, that serves double duty.

LOCATIONS

The first places to put scratching posts are where your cats may already be inappropriately scratching. When locating posts, keep two things in mind: (1) territories, and (2) where your cats like to scratch. In regard to territories, spread out the posts enough so every cat will feel comfortable using them. Just as you've placed the litter boxes in various parts of the home to address territorial boundaries, you'll scatter the scratching posts. If it isn't in your budget to buy several vertical posts, or if you aren't sure about certain locations, scatter a few of the corrugated cardboard scratchers around.

As for where your cats like to scratch, there are a couple of common areas to cover. It's a pretty safe bet that scratching posts placed by common eating and sleeping areas will get used. There's nothing like a good stretch after being curled up while napping or hunched over the food bowl.

Some cats scratch doorways or furniture near room entrances as a way to mark their turf. If that's the case with your cats, place posts in those areas so those kitties can comfortably mark their territory perimeters. Don't put the post in the back corner of a room if a cat's preference is to mark upon first entering a room.

If a cat is spraying in a certain area, in addition to the behavior modification described in chapter 7, you can place a scratching post in the room to help dissolve the stress she associates with that area.

For cats who get concerned about company coming through the front door, place a post right inside the entrance, or near where they supervise new arrivals.

If there's an area where the cats tend to spend much of their time, place a couple of posts and/or scratching pads in the center of the room as well as near furniture and walls. Some cats may like being out of the main flow of traffic, but others may feel more comfortable right in the center of the room. This may also help maintain peace within the hierarchy because the subordinate cats can remain in their comfort zones and the higher-ranking cats can command the central area.

FURNITURE SCRATCHING

A cat will choose a piece of furniture if there isn't a better alternative for her. When looking for a scratching surface, a cat chooses a sturdy object with an appealing texture and a convenient location. A couch or chairs are common targets because they're tall, so a cat can get a good stretch, and the material allows the cat to dig in her nails and rake them down the surface. Also, the location of furniture is often ideal from a cat's point of view.

Since scratching is an innate behavior, you can't prevent it by scolding, hitting, squirting water, or chasing. They will still want to scratch. If you try to prevent it, the cat will find other locations for scratching and will become increasingly anxious. You may think reprimanding works because the cat runs whenever she sees you. You may be convinced that the cat "knows she's being bad," but what's actually happening is that the cat now associates your presence with fear and anxiety. She's running because her relationship with you has deteriorated—not because you have her well trained. Since the cat needs to scratch, every time she has the desire, she will now feel highly anxious. That only leads her to want to scratch more for displacement, or groom to relieve her frustration. Either way, the cat isn't happy.

To correct scratching on inappropriate objects, you need a twofold approach: an *effective deterrent* and a *better alternative*. That way, you're turning a negative into a positive and allowing your cats to engage in this natural and vital aspect of their lives.

CATWISE CAUTION

If you come home and find a newly scratched area on the furniture, don't bring your cat over to it for punishment. She'll have no idea why you're acting this way and may become afraid of you.

DETERRENTS AND ALTERNATIVES You've probably tried aluminum foil and deterrent sprays and have come to the realization that they don't work. Sticky Paws, which I mentioned earlier as a way to keep cats off counters, is a double-sided transparent tape made specifically to deter furniture scratching. It comes in strips that you place over the area of the couch where the cat is scratching. The tape's adhesive won't leave a residue, so it's better than plain double-sided tape. Sticky Paws also comes in an extra-wide size, which is great for window screens and large areas of furniture.

Cover the scratched areas of the furniture with Sticky Paws, and make sure the humans in your family know the tape is in place so nobody leans against it.

If the scratched area of the couch or chair is too massive to cover with the tape, then you'll have to cover the entire piece with a sheet. Tuck the sheet in all around and tape or safety pin it at the bottom so cats can't get up underneath. You can also place some strips of Sticky Paws on the sheet over areas where cats may still try to gain access.

Now that you've set up the deterrent, you need to give the cat a better option and it has to be not only appealing, but also convenient. Place the scratching post right next to the piece of furniture that was being scratched. In order to shift the cat's focus to the post, the alternative has to be obvious. The cat will walk over to the couch and discover that her usual scratching surface is no longer appealing. Instead of having to search for an alternative, she'll find this incredible scratching post right there. You can even rub a little catnip on the post for extra incentive. Leave the Sticky Paws in place until you're sure the cat has been retrained to the post.

If a cat is horizontally scratching an area of carpet, place the scratching pad right over that spot. If the cat moves the pad to get to the carpet, put a heavy-duty carpet runner down (the kind with the nubby underside so it doesn't slide) and then place scratching pads on top and around the area. Even though a cat may be horizontally scratching the carpet, you may want to offer a vertical post as well as a horizontal pad. She may have been scratching the carpet because it was the only effective texture. However, it may actually be the *location* the cat preferred.

WHEN TO REPLACE POSTS

Posts such as those by TopCat should hold up for a long, long time. Rope-wrapped posts may eventually loosen over time, and you'll just need to tighten them up. You shouldn't have to worry about replacing vertical posts very often. Even with the rope-wrapped ones, if the post is well made, you can replace the rope rather than buy a whole new one. The corrugated cardboard scratching pads can usually be flipped over, so you'll get double the use out of them. You can even buy replacement inserts when these are completely demolished.

When you do get to the point of wanting to replace a post, buy the new one and place it next to the old one. Let the cats start using the new one before you get rid of the old one. This way, they'll have time to get comfortable with it and leave enough of their visual and olfactory marks on it to know its their post. If you're just going to rewrap a rope-covered post or flip over a corrugated cardboard pad, rub a little catnip on it for enticement and to ease the cats over the "newness" of it.

A NOTE ABOUT DECLAWING

If you get the right kind of scratching posts, put them in good locations, and set up the appropriate deterrents, you shouldn't have a furniture-scratching problem. If you still do, then one of the elements hasn't been done correctly yet.

Declawing is a very controversial topic. I never recommend declawing. Sadly, for many misinformed owners, it has become as routine as vaccinations. The declawing procedure is actually an amputation of the top joints of the toes. Recovery is extremely painful, and some cats remain sensitive about their paws long after the initial healing period. If pain medication isn't administered after surgery, the recovery is even more difficult. Declawing takes away the cat's first line of defense should she ever escape outside. It also hinders her ability to escape from an attacker. Scratching is such a vital part of a cat's physical and psychological well-being that it's tragic when it's taken away needlessly.

If you're thinking of declawing your cats to protect human family members in the home, remember that a cat can still bite if backed into a corner. Nothing is as important as proper training of both feline and human family members, supervision of children, and making sure everyone (four-legged and two-legged) is safe.

If you have one or more declawed cats and you're adding a new cat into the environment, you may be thinking she'll have to be declawed as well to even the playing field, but that's not so. Keep the new cat's nails trimmed regularly, and she'll be fine. Do a proper introduction, and you shouldn't have any problems. Declawed cats and those with intact claws can safely share a home.

Aggression

ggression is very frightening for owners, whether directed at another cat or at humans. Intercat aggression is scary enough, but when the cat you love suddenly turns on *you*, it puts the whole household in crisis because of the risk of injury—especially if you have children. Cat bites can be serious, and aggression is a problem that must be diagnosed and dealt with correctly so no one gets hurt.

As frightening as it is, feline aggression is a normal response to a threatening situation in the animal world. While you certainly don't want it displayed in your home, keep in mind that it's not an abnormal behavior. In a free-roaming environment, cats fight for territory, mates, and for defense of the nest and their rank in the colony. Even the hunt for food requires aggression. For kitties, aggressive behavior is a form of communication and not your cat's attempt to be mean or spiteful. To solve the problem, you have to uncover what the cat is saying through his behavior.

In animals, aggression is either offensive or defensive. But in most cases, cats would rather avoid actual conflict, and that's why they have such an elaborate repertoire of postures and vocalizations. It's definitely to the cat's advantage not to engage in a battle that might leave him injured and unable to capture prey. In a cat-dense environment such as a multicat home or crowded suburban neighborhood, territories are small and some cats feel they are left with no other option.

Common aggressive displays between cats mostly involve posturing. This allows the cat to work within the hierarchy structure: a subordinate will back down much of the time.

Offensive feline aggression is demonstrated by a cat approaching the potential threat, obviously narrowing the distance between himself and the opponent while displaying an intimidating posture. The defensive cat is trying to increase the distance and is focused on avoidance.

Familiar cats may frequently experience covert aggression. No active physical battles may take place if the cats recognize they aren't equal in status. The dominant cat's various markings often effectively keep the lower-ranking cat continuously intimidated. Covert aggression can also occur when a new cat is introduced into the home. Any of the kitties may not feel confident enough to engage in active aggression, so passive methods are used to check things out.

Underlying medical causes that could contribute to aggressive behavior must be ruled out before assuming this is a behavioral problem. A physical exam and appropriate lab work must be done. Cats with conditions such as hyperthyroidism, hyperesthesia and epilepsy can display aggressive behavior. A cat in physical pain can display aggression when handled. There are also several other medical conditions that can contribute. The onset of social maturity at about two to four years of age can trigger episodes of aggression as cats jockey for elevated status in the pecking order.

If there's an unsolvable litter box problem, you have to look at potential underlying aggression as well.

Since aggression can lead to injury to animals and people in the home, seek out the help of your veterinarian. He or she will be able to rule out potential medical causes and help you uncover the reason for the behavior. Depending on the severity of the problem, you may be referred to a behaviorist, and drug therapy may be required during behavior modification. Don't try to treat an aggression problem without help, especially if you don't know the cause.

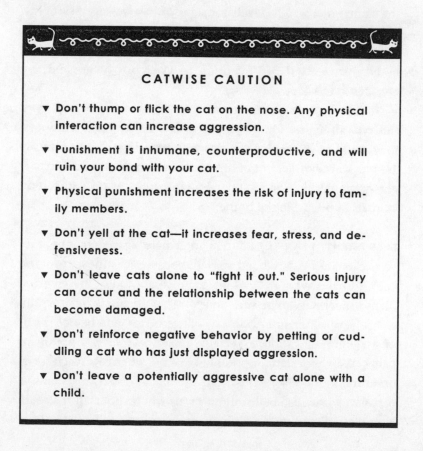

CATWISE CAUTION

▼ Don't thump or flick the cat on the nose. Any physical interaction can increase aggression.

▼ Punishment is inhumane, counterproductive, and will ruin your bond with your cat.

▼ Physical punishment increases the risk of injury to family members.

▼ Don't yell at the cat—it increases fear, stress, and defensiveness.

▼ Don't leave cats alone to "fight it out." Serious injury can occur and the relationship between the cats can become damaged.

▼ Don't reinforce negative behavior by petting or cuddling a cat who has just displayed aggression.

▼ Don't leave a potentially aggressive cat alone with a child.

INTERCAT (INTERMALE) AGGRESSION

Testosterone is a big factor in aggressive behavior between male cats. Toms commonly fight for territory and available females. Neutering will likely eliminate the behavior, especially if it's done when the cat reaches sexual maturity at six to seven months, or at least before he becomes a year old.

The onset of social maturity can spark intercat aggression in a home where the cats have previously coexisted peacefully. If you have a couple of cats who are reaching social maturity at about the same time, watch closely for signs of passive aggression. Just because the behaviors may not include hissing, growling, or outright physical battles doesn't mean there isn't a standoff. Watch body postures and pay attention to litter box habits and any changes in territory.

A cat who isn't a member of your household can also spark this type of aggression. If you allow any of your cats outdoors, they could be getting into battles with roaming cats. If your cats are indoor only, the sight of an unfamiliar outdoor cat could trigger spray-marking or redirected aggression toward companion animals or people in the home.

TREATMENT PLAN To address intermale aggression, be sure your cats are neutered and spayed, because it is most common among males who are looking for mates. Modify the environment if necessary to be sure everyone has adequate territory. Increase vertical territory, add extra litter boxes, and be observant of cat communication, especially if you have several dominant males. Watch for signs of potential trouble when cats reach social maturity. Put a bell on the collar of the cat displaying offensive behavior so you can better monitor his whereabouts. It'll also inhibit his ability to stalk the victim and may give other cats a little more warning time. Separate aggressive cats while you figure out the underlying cause of the behavior. Depending upon the severity of the problem, you may have to do a total reintroduction as described later in this chapter. Keep in mind that, in some cases, there are cats who simply cannot coexist together and must remain permanently separated.

Cats allowed outdoors can return home in an agitated state and behave aggressively toward companion cats. Keep your cats indoors to prevent conflicts with other outdoor cats and any redirected aggression once they return home. If the intercat aggression between companions is caused by the appearance of an unfamiliar cat outside, follow the instructions in the section of this chapter under "Redirected Aggression."

FEAR AGGRESSION

A frightened cat's first choice will be to avoid potential conflict altogether and escape. If he can't escape, or feels backed into a corner, a cat may resort to aggression. First, he will display a defensive body posture: an arched back with his hair standing on end at first and then a crouch with ears rotated back and flattened against the head. His pupils will be dilated and he will probably growl, hiss, and perhaps spit. He may even be caught between two positions at once. His upper body and front feet may face forward, ready to do battle if necessary, but his hindquarters may face sideways, ready to help him bolt at the first opportunity for escape. He will stay in the defensive posture until escape becomes possible or the opponent retreats.

A cat who wasn't exposed to various stimuli as a kitten (such as unfamiliar places, noises, being handled by the veterinarian, visitors in the home, and so forth) may exhibit this behavior more frequently. This is also a common display when the cat takes the dreaded trip to the veterinarian. Animal hospital staff are all too familiar with the tightly wound, razor blade–wielding furball crouched at the far end of the examination table. I was once a veterinary technician, and I know firsthand that there's nothing fun about taking the temperature of a scared and aggressive cat. It doesn't matter what kind of high-tech instant-read thermometer you use, the cat is going to do his best to make sure you and that thermometer stay the heck away from any of his body parts!

If the person or animal opponent continues to advance and no immediate means of escape becomes available, the frightened cat will roll from his initial posture into the belly-up position for full defense. The cat may consider the approaching person or animal as a threat in the future as well. You can help your cat with some of this fear by making sure children and cat-loving visitors are respectful of the cat's personal space and don't continue to advance when a cat assumes a fearful position. Teach children how to interpret basic cat body language so they'll know not to approach a crouched cat and not to back one into a corner.

TREATMENT PLAN If the behavior is limited to the veterinary visit, use a carrier that comes apart so the cat can stay in the bottom of it while he is examined. Sometimes being able to stay in the familiar carrier will lessen a cat's anxiety. At home, before placing the cat in the carrier for the trip to the veterinarian, spray the inside corners with Feliway. You can also bring Feliway with you to the clinic and spray the exam table before placing the cat on it. You can find more information on Feliway in chapter 7. Schedule veterinary appointments at off-peak times when you won't have so much of a wait. Unless you can't help it, avoid Saturday appointments.

Be aware of how much restraint your cat needs during veterinary exams. Obviously the staff members need to be safe, but in some cases, less is more. Muzzles and restraint bags/cages can actually intensify the cat's fear. In extreme cases, your veterinarian may prescribe acepromazine to be given to your cat at home before the appointment. Sometimes your cat may need an inhaled anesthetic to sedate him slightly during the exam. A mask is placed over the cat's mouth and nose so he can breathe in a mild anesthetic. It's very short acting, and once the mask is removed, the cat will come around very quickly.

For fear aggression in a cage environment such as during hospitalization or boarding, place an open paper bag on its side in the corner of the cage. Roll the edge of the bag into a cuff so it stays open and doesn't collapse. The cat will calm down much more quickly if he is allowed to stay out of sight. You can also tape a sheet of newspaper over the front of the cage to help him feel more secure.

If fear aggression occurs at home, allow the cat to calm down, either isolated in a darkened room or just left alone where he is. While he's still tense and reactive, the less interaction the better. If you're worried about the safety of the fearful cat, you can set up baby gates in a doorway. Stack two or three baby gates—one on top of another—or temporarily install an inexpensive screen door.

If the problem involves only children or a particular person, use gradual desensitization and counterconditioning. Have the person sit quietly at one end of the room while you offer the cat treats or dinner on the other side of the room. You can also conduct an interactive play session. Just be sure you allow the cat to stay well within his comfort zone. Gradually, over a number of sessions, you can have the person inch closer. If the problem is another cat, you can help the kitties associate each other with positive experiences by feeding them in each other's presence. Keep the food bowls on opposite sides of the room and if the cats eat without a problem, you can inch the bowls closer in future sessions. If one cat refuses to eat, you've moved too fast and the bowls are too close together. Treats can also help them make positive associations. Basically, it all comes down to bribery.

If the aggression is more severe and caused by stalking and attacking by another cat, a reintroduction should be done. If the cat is afraid of all the other cats in the home and a reintroduction with appropriate medication hasn't helped, a separate area may need to be permanently set up for the cat.

Sometimes when the reintroduction doesn't work and triggers an attack the second the cats see each other, you can try keeping them apart for weeks (yes, weeks). In that time, work on leash and harness training with the offensively aggressive cat. This will give you more control, but can be used only if the cat is *completely* comfortable with the leash. If he's not, you'll create more of a problem and you risk getting injured yourself.

If you notice a standoff taking place between your cats or if an outright battle is under way, make a noise to interrupt the behavior and give the victim a chance to escape. *Do not,* under any circumstances, attempt physically to break up the fight. You would risk serious injury.

Don't overlook changes you can make to the environment in order to allow for more escape routes and break up patterns of fear aggression.

TERRITORIAL AGGRESSION

This type of aggression may rear its fuzzy little head when a cat reaches social maturity. It can be directed toward animals or people and it may be demonstrated toward specific cats in the home but not toward others.

When a new cat is introduced into a home where there are existing cats, you'll often see territorial aggression. It can also occur between longtime companions when one cat returns from the veterinary clinic, because the unfamiliar, and definitely unpopular, scents can make him smell like an intruder.

Territorial aggression can be exhibited in various subtle ways. It may happen in your home without your even hearing a hiss or seeing a paw raised. For example, a dominant cat may block access to the litter boxes or the food bowl, but it may look to you as if he's just casually lounging in the doorway. You may not have any idea this blocking behavior is taking place until an inappropriate elimination or spray-marking problem becomes obvious.

TREATMENT PLAN Since cats live within a hierarchy, you have to be observant and watch for hints that territorial aggression is bubbling under the surface. The proper introduction of a new cat, or a reintroduction of current resident cats, if necessary, is the most important foundation. Make sure there are an adequate number of litter boxes in various territories around the house, as well as multiple feeding stations. Increase vertical territory and create various levels to help the cats maintain a peaceful pecking order.

If the problem is triggered by a visit to the veterinarian, put the cat in a separate room when he first comes home so he'll have a chance to groom and smell like himself again. It'll also help him quiet down after the ordeal and get back to normal behavior. You can also take a towel and *first* rub the cats who stayed home and then rub the returning cat. Don't do it the other way around because it will spread the scents from veterinary clinic and you'll have a house full of angry cats. If you repeatedly have a problem with territorial aggression after a veterinary visit, rub the cat down with a towel before leaving and then use that towel again on the cat when he returns home.

Sometimes, no matter what you try, there are just some cats

who can't coexist peacefully. In that case you have to modify the living arrangements so they can remain separated, or consider re-homing a cat who might be happier in a single-cat environment.

PLAY AGGRESSION

Play aggression tends to be directed toward people. Cats who were taken away from their mothers and littermates too early, or hand-raised orphan cats, may not know how to gauge their play response because they didn't experience social play with litter-mates as kittens. They may cross the line and play too aggres-sively with you and may not have learned to keep their claws retracted during play.

You can also unintentionally bring about this behavior if you use inappropriate play techniques with the cat when he is a kit-ten. Although it can be tempting to use your wiggling fingers to entice a kitten to play, it sends a bad message that can have seri-ous implications as he grows. If he learns that biting his owner's hand is acceptable, he'll also think it's okay to bite your young child's hand or that of your elderly grandmother. Hands should never be used as toys.

You also want to avoid wrestling-type play with your cat be-cause it can cause a defensive response.

TREATMENT PLAN Watch for signs that the cat is moving from play mode into aggression—such as flattening of the ears and growling. Use interactive fishing pole toys when you play with your cat so he gets a clear message concerning what is acceptable to bite. Small toys don't put enough distance between your hand and the cat's teeth. Use treats to reward the cat when he plays ap-propriately. Schedule two or three play sessions a day so the cat doesn't develop pent-up energy, and don't engage in wrestling, roughhousing, or teasing.

If the cat still goes for your hand or ambushes your ankles when you walk into a room, you may have to use aversion therapy. Carry a water pistol or can of compressed air (the kind used for cleaning photo equipment). Use the smallest squirt of air or water necessary to interrupt the behavior. Don't spray the cat's face, but give a quick squirt to his side or back end. The point is to startle the cat mildly and break the behavior pattern—don't terrify him. Never spray a cat in the face, especially if using compressed air. It's also important not to let him see that the blast came from you so he'll think it was one of those "acts of God." Aversion techniques must be used carefully, or the cat may become afraid of you. Punishment should never be used.

In a single-cat household, adding a second cat of complementary temperament may also help. For example, if your cat is very assertive, try to chose a companion cat who doesn't appear too dominant. If your resident cat is very shy, you wouldn't want to pair him up with a feline bulldozer. If your kitty is a lap cat, it's nice to match him up with a cat who doesn't appear to be a lap cat.

Even though play aggression tends to be directed toward people, be aware of the reaction of other cats in the home. If a kitty is being rough with you, it might intimidate others, and they may be reluctant to get involved in any group play. Also, if a cat stays revved up from inappropriately playing with you, he might be less than pleasant to unsuspecting companion cats afterward.

REDIRECTED AGGRESSION

Redirected aggression results from a cat being cut off from the primary source of his agitation, so he turns his aggression on the

nearest cat, person, or dog. The agitated cat is in such a highly reactive state that he doesn't realize at whom he's lashing out.

The most typical example of redirected aggression happens
when a cat looks out of the window and spots an unfamiliar cat in
the yard. He becomes agitated and highly frustrated. A companion cat walks by or jumps up on the window to join him, totally
unaware of his agitation, and instantly becomes the target of the
agitated kitty. A surprise attack like this can damage the close relationship between two cats—especially between close companions. Other situations that are potential triggers include the scent
of an unfamiliar cat on your clothes, a sudden loud noise, being in
an unfamiliar environment, or an owner's trying physically to
break up a cat fight. Redirected aggression usually doesn't last too
long, but it may continue when fueled by the ongoing defensive
posture of the attacked cat. All of a sudden the two cats no longer
recognize each other as friends because of the hostile posturing.

Redirected aggression is often misdiagnosed as unprovoked
aggression because an owner is unaware of the primary cause.
After seeing a cat outdoors, your indoor cat can stay highly reactive for hours, so by the time you come home from work, the
outdoor cat is long gone and the only evidence you see is a very
hostile cat going after his companions.

TREATMENT PLAN Separate the cats immediately. If you can
coax the aggressor into another room safely, then do so without
picking him up. Otherwise, remove the other animals. The
sooner you separate the cats, the quicker things will get back to
normal, and the risk of long-term damage to the cats' relationships will be greatly reduced. Even if you only suspect redirected
aggression, separate the cats. Leave the agitated cat alone until
he calms down and resumes normal activity—eating, using the lit-

ter box, normal (not displacement) grooming, napping. Darken the room and keep it quiet. Turn off the TV or radio. Use Feliway in the environment to help restore calm. When you reintroduce the cats again, do it under positive circumstances such as offering a meal or treats. Don't be in a rush to reintroduce them—make sure everyone is calm and back to normal.

If you can identify the initial stimulus, eliminate or modify it. For instance, if you know the cause to be an outdoor cat, block your cats' view by covering the bottom half of the windows with white poster paper. The half-blocked windows will allow light to enter and your cats to enjoy watching birds in the trees. The outdoor cat may move on to another yard if he can't see your cats through the blocked windows. Discourage the outdoor cat by making a loud noise whenever you see him. You can also keep a long-range water pistol near the door. If a neighbor owns the cat, perhaps you can explain the situation and convince him to keep his cat indoors. This can be a very touchy subject for people, and you don't want to ruin neighbor relations, but if you think he may be reasonable about it, give it a try. If you suspect the cat is a stray, you can try trapping him. If you don't think you can do this yourself, contact your local shelter because they may have a list of people who can help you. Perhaps there's even a feline rescue organization in your area.

If you have bird feeders outdoors and they're attracting unwanted cats into the yard, you may have to remove the feeders. If you want to keep feeding the birds, place the feeders where your cats can't see them and make it up to them by playing a cat entertainment video or DVD on a regular basis. The videos showcase wildlife such as birds, squirrels, fish, mice, and so forth. You can find them in pet supply stores, through mail-order companies, and online. My cats love them!

PAIN-INDUCED AGGRESSION

Pair-induced aggression is a defensive reaction that can occur when the cat's tail is pulled or when a child grabs a fistful of fur. It can also be caused by an injury or underlying medical condition, as in the case of an arthritic cat who may experience pain when handled.

Social play during kittenhood is important because it teaches cats how much pressure to use when biting so as not to inflict pain. The reaction of the kitten he bites becomes a valuable lesson. Cats raised without littermates miss this lesson and, as adults, may bite too hard when playing with a feline companion and end up on the receiving end of pain-induced aggression.

Sometimes pain-induced aggression can turn into a secondary problem of fear aggression. For example, a cat with a chronic painful ear infection may display pain-induced aggression initially and then after it's healed, the memory of the pain may cause him to display fear aggression when the ear is touched.

Abuse—either malicious or unintentional (such as by children)—can also cause pain-induced aggression.

TREATMENT PLAN Obviously the first course of action is to alleviate the pain as much as possible. In the case of chronic pain, teach all family members how to handle the cat carefully to minimize the pain. Even though it may be difficult, you mustn't reward a cat for aggression even if it's pain induced. Behavior modification may be needed if the cat's pain-induced aggression has developed into fear aggression.

PETTING-INDUCED AGGRESSION

Let me set the scene. You're sitting on the couch, watching your favorite TV show. Your cat is curled up in your lap and you're lovingly petting him. At the end of a long day, this is the perfect way for you to relax. Suddenly, like a bolt of lightning, your cat whips his head around and sinks his teeth into your hand hard enough to draw blood. Then he leaps from your lap and sits on the floor a few feet away, grooming himself as you stare in disbelief at your injured hand and wonder what the heck just happened. The behavior displayed is called petting-induced aggression, and although you may think the attack came out of nowhere, or that your kitty became momentarily possessed, in reality, he probably did give you warning signs before the attack.

Some cats initially enjoy being petted but then reach a definite tolerance threshold. The cause of this type of aggression may be overstimulation or temporary contact confusion as the cat gets drowsy. When the cat gets sleepy and then feels something coming in contact with his body, his survival instinct may take over and he might bite or scratch in defense. Petting-induced aggression may also be part of a dominance issue as well (see the following section on "Status-Related Aggression"). Some cats are also very particular about where on the body they are petted. Some may not like being stroked down the back, along the sides, or near the tail.

Although you may think this behavior is unprovoked, the cat will give you body language signals and sometimes vocalizations as well. Warning signs may include skin rippling, tail lashing or thumping, shifting body position, tense posture, rotated-backward ears, low growling, cessation of purring. The cat's whiskers may also rotate forward and fan out before the attack. From the cat's point of view, he is giving plenty of notice that he's no longer enjoying being petted. When he feels he has no choice, that's when he bites.

TREATMENT PLAN The best way to handle this problem is to pet for shorter periods. If you know the cat can tolerate only two or

three minutes of petting, stop after one minute. To break the behavior pattern, always leave the cat wanting more. If you don't
know the cat's limit, watch for warning signals as you pet him.
It's better just to give a quick pet and be content to let him
merely sit on your lap. When you do pet him, stick to areas you
know he enjoys. This positive experience will help him change
his association with the situation. Over time you may be able
gradually to increase the length of the petting session, but it's important to respect your cat's limits.

STATUS-RELATED AGGRESSION

A dominant cat can display the same type of behavior toward
you that he does toward other cats in the home without affecting
his rank in the hierarchy.

The cat might bite or scratch in order to be in control. He may
bite when lifted off a table or moved from a chair, when you try
to pet him, or even when you simply walk by. He may exhibit this
behavior only to certain members of the family or to visitors in
the home.

Other examples of status-related aggression include blocking
an owner's path, direct stares, and head rubbing an owner only to
back up and stare as a challenge. The cat may also accept affection
only if he is the one to initiate it. Mouthing behavior is also possible where he puts his teeth on you without actually biting down.

TREATMENT PLAN Watch for body language signals—flattened
ears, direct stare, growling, tense body posture. If the cat is on
your lap and starts growling, staring you down, or mouthing
your arm, stand up so he is released to the floor. Don't place him
on the floor with your hands because you'll surely get bitten.
Stand up and let him fall safely to the floor so he learns his be-

havior doesn't give him the control he wants. Don't interact with the cat until he has resumed normal behavior. Don't hit or punish him because it's inhumane and also will be viewed as a challenge and will compound the problem. Correct him at the first sign of the behavior. Again, watch body language. A water pistol will help only if you are able to catch the behavior immediately. If the cat is blocking your path, walk past him so he knows that blocking isn't an acceptable behavior. Watch for signs that he might lunge at you, so have your water pistol ready to deter him if necessary.

Use of clicker training may also help these cats to learn what type of behavior is acceptable. You can get a clicker at a pet supply store. Click the instant the cat does what you want and immediately offer a food reward. The clicker helps the cat make the immediate connection with having done something good since he'll associate the sound with the upcoming food reward.

Speaking of food, feed the cat on a schedule rather than free-choice so his meals will be earned and he'll make the connection that they come from you.

Cats who display status-related aggression may never become marshmallow lap cats. You have to be content with just having the cat sit on your lap or by your side.

PREDATORY AGGRESSION

Predatory *behavior* toward appropriate targets (toys, real prey) is different from predatory *aggression* directed toward a person's body part (usually the feet or hands). Predatory aggression simulates a hunt: silent approach, body and head low to the ground, and then the swift pounce. The problem occurs when this behavior is directed toward you. You may be a target as you get out of bed in the morning and the cat pounces on your moving feet. He

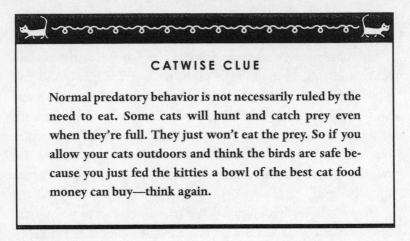

CATWISE CLUE

Normal predatory behavior is not necessarily ruled by the need to eat. Some cats will hunt and catch prey even when they're full. They just won't eat the prey. So if you allow your cats outdoors and think the birds are safe because you just fed the kitties a bowl of the best cat food money can buy—think again.

may also slink around following you, then pounce whenever you make a sudden movement.

TREATMENT PLAN The cat needs adequate outlets to satisfy his prey drive. Conduct interactive play sessions on a daily basis so the cat can appropriately engage his prey drive as he learns what is and isn't an acceptable target. Additionally, you can put a bell on the cat's collar during training so you'll be more aware of his location.

MATERNAL AGGRESSION

Queens (mother cats) may show aggression toward people or other animals as they protect their nests. They'll do a lot of warning (growling, posturing) to keep intruders at a very far distance from the babies. Unfamiliar people and cats who post a potential threat are most often targeted.

Don't underestimate the threat of a queen. She *will* attack in order to protect her babies.

In free-roaming situations, there's a risk of infanticide by male cats. Even an indoor queen may become aggressive to any of the males in your home, depending on whether they previously had a hostile relationship or not. As the kittens grow, the intensity of the aggression lessens.

TREATMENT PLAN Keep the nest safe from the other cats in the home. It's often necessary to set up a "nursery" for them in one room of your home where you can keep the door closed. Provide a litter box in there, a scratching post for the mother, as well as food and water. You can place a boxed lined with butcher's paper, which is cleaner than newspaper, in the closet or behind a piece of furniture—wherever the mother seems to want her nest. Cut a U shape in one side of the box so it's easy for the queen to go in and out. If you suspect any of your male cats may try to harm the kittens, be very careful when going in and out of the room to make sure no one sneaks by you.

To reduce the risk of maternal aggression, avoid handling the kittens for the first several days after birth and then handle only on a very limited basis for the first two weeks (begin daily socialization after two weeks). Early handling before two weeks should be restricted to family members with whom the mother cat is very comfortable.

IDIOPATHIC AGGRESSION

This is totally and truly unprovoked aggression that seems to have no known cause.

All other possible causes of aggression must first be ruled out, including those often misdiagnosed, such as redirected aggression. Underlying medical causes must be ruled out. For example, hyperesthesia may actually be the cause of what seems to be totally unprovoked aggression. Hyperesthesia is often referred to as rolling skin disease. This syndrome presents in a few different ways: a super-sensitivity apparently develops along the back and tail, which causes the cat to excessively groom. That often progresses to the cat attacking himself or self-mutilation. Totally unprovoked aggression is another symptom of this syndrome. The cat may appear fine one minute, but when touched he turns very aggressive. Seizures can be associated with this syndrome as well.

Idiopathic aggression is rare. It's difficult to diagnose and difficult to treat. Almost all aggressive behaviors can be traced back to one of the previous categories.

TREATMENT PLAN This is far too difficult for an owner to try to correct. You must have the cat seen by the veterinarian for all appropriate diagnostic workups and then seek the help of a behavior specialist.

LEARNED AGGRESSION

Learned aggression is a subcategory that can apply to any of the categories listed in this chapter.

Learned aggression can occur when the owner inadvertently reinforces a cat's aggressive behavior. If you attempt to soothe or cuddle a cat displaying aggression, it can actually reinforce the pattern. It's a common mistake made by owners because they want to comfort an upset cat, but it actually will send a message that he's acting appropriately. He'll react that way again in the future under the same circumstances. On the other hand, you don't want to punish a cat for being aggressive. This is where it's important to be familiar with your cat's body language, anticipate what might be an aggression trigger for him, and use appropriate behavior modification techniques as described in this chapter and earlier in this book. If you recognize early warning signs in the cat's body language that tell you he's starting to get tense, that's the time to use distraction to keep him calm. Anything that creates a positive reinforcement must be done *before* the actual unwanted behavior is displayed. Remember, positive reinforcement is a message that tells the cat you like what he's doing. People can also create learned aggression in cats through teasing, provoking, or physical punishment.

REINTRODUCTIONS

You're probably scratching your head at this one, wondering what the heck this is and why you'd need to do it. A reintroduction is simply starting from scratch and introducing familiar cats as if they'd never met. The process may not take as long as a true first-time introduction, though in the case of serious aggression between cats it can take even longer. Whatever time frame is needed, the technique will basically be the same.

There are a few situations that suggest you need to do a reintroduction. For example, if you incorrectly introduced a new cat into your existing cat community and things have never settled down, it's best to just start all over again. Very commonly there are circumstances that may come up in which cats who previously got along beautifully may suddenly become archenemies. It can happen, for example, when an episode of redirected aggression continues to cycle around because the attacked cat becomes defensive, or a cat reaches social maturity and starts to test the waters of elevated status.

When you're dealing with cats who are constantly after each other, the more you keep trudging onward without progress, the more the negative relationships become cemented. The reintroduction allows the cats to get a much-needed breather from each other so the stress level can go down. Then, once everyone seems back to normal, you can begin the reintro process and help the cats rediscover what they previously liked about each other or get to like each other for the first time. No matter how badly the initial introduction went or how long the cats have been together, the reintro method is your best shot at correcting the problem so the cats can start to live peacefully. How slowly or meticulously you'll have to do each step will vary depending on your situation, but I'd advise you to err on the side of caution.

The one major difference between a new cat introduction and a reintroduction is *location*. If one cat is bullying another cat, it's best to separate the cats in a way that gives the victim the choice location of the house. You don't want to isolate the victim in a less choice area and give the aggressor the run of the house because getting the results he wanted will just reinforce his behavior. He'll think his aggressive display scared off the victim, and you may end up with even more of a bully on your hands. The victim cat will also benefit from having access to the premium areas because it may boost his confidence and level of security.

Sometimes, though, it just doesn't work out to separate the aggressor into one area if he gets too worked up or frustrated. Also, sometimes the victim is just too terrified and feels more secure in a sanctuary room. You have to customize the separation details to fit your individual cats.

Before beginning the reintroduction you need to work on a little confidence boosting for the victim and a little anger management for the aggressor. The interactive play will help the victim start to feel safe and relaxed enough to engage his prey drive. If the aggression repeatedly took place in particular areas of the home, conduct his sessions in those locations to help change his mind-set. It takes confidence for a cat to be a predator, so one hopes these play sessions will bring out his more confident side.

Playing at the scene of the crime will also create a new positive association with that area. You can also offer treats there, and don't forget to use Feliway in those areas. If the victim feels more comfortable in the sanctuary room, then keep the play in there for now. After a little while, you should be able to open the door and entice her out with the toys. Make sure the other cat is safely away in another room; then let the victim cat set the pace of expanding her comfort zone.

For the aggressor, his separation into a less-than-premium area of the house shouldn't be a punishment. Don't banish him to the basement. His area should be inviting and cozy but not restricted to the specific areas for which he was fighting. Engage him in several daily play sessions to help him learn what are acceptable targets for biting. Use Feliway in his environment. When both cats seem calm and ready, you can begin the reintroduction, which is described under "New Cat Introductions" in chapter 4.

Before the cats are out of their confined areas and together again, keep an eye out for potential situations in the environment that could trigger another problem. For example, if you previously had one community food bowl, the cats may benefit from having more than one feeding station. Make sure everyone has access to the litter boxes, favorite perches, or napping hideaways. Be observant of which situations seem to create tension between the cats so you can get in there and make modifications.

Another important tool in your behavior modification toolbox will be the use of positive diversion techniques to diffuse potential confrontations. See chapter 5 for specifics.

WHAT TO DO IF YOU ARE BITTEN

The three most important rules to follow to avoid being on the receiving end of a cat bite are these: (1) pay attention to the cat's body language; (2) don't use your hands as toys; and (3) don't physically punish a cat.

Even if you follow those rules, you still may find yourself with a cat's teeth embedded in your hand. How you handle the situation at that point is crucial to minimize injury to yourself and to prevent the cat from suffering additional stress.

The first mistake is to try to pull away from the cat. It's a natural reaction, but it's a mistake because you then are behaving like prey and the cat may bite down harder. It's his natural response when he feels something tugging to get out of his grasp. Instead of pulling away, gently push *toward* his mouth and this will loosen his grip. This momentarily confuses him because prey would never voluntarily move in the direction of the predator. When he has loosened his grip, you can quickly remove your hand. At the moment that the cat bites, you should also use your voice to startle him. Let out a high-pitched "ouch" (the word will come naturally, along with a few other more colorful ones, I'm sure). The sudden high-pitched sound will startle and confuse him.

If the cat was biting in play and got carried away, or if he thought he was biting the toy and you moved your hand at the wrong time, redirect him toward the toy and be ready to praise him when he plays appropriately. If he was biting out of aggression, try to figure out what triggered it. If you're dealing with a cat who is prone to biting, keep a water pistol or can of compressed air handy at all times during training. You can use either of these to startle the cat when he first shows signs of aggressive behavior. Use the smallest amount of stimulus to startle him and interrupt the behavior. This technique must be used humanely and correctly or you'll risk creating more of a problem.

Finally, don't forget to reward the cat for good behavior. You can't just keep training him what *not* to do—you have to let him know what you *do* want as well. During the training process,

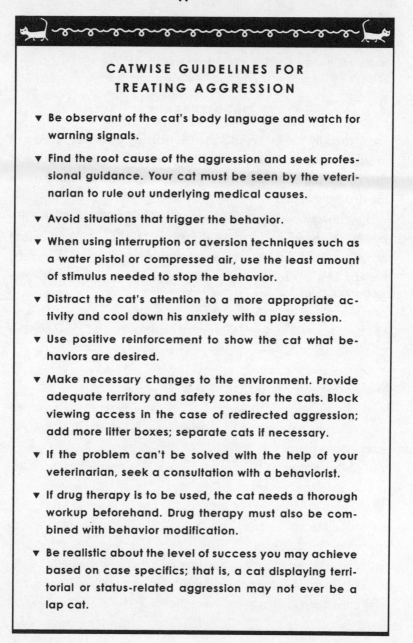

CATWISE GUIDELINES FOR
TREATING AGGRESSION

▼ Be observant of the cat's body language and watch for warning signals.

▼ Find the root cause of the aggression and seek professional guidance. Your cat must be seen by the veterinarian to rule out underlying medical causes.

▼ Avoid situations that trigger the behavior.

▼ When using interruption or aversion techniques such as a water pistol or compressed air, use the least amount of stimulus needed to stop the behavior.

▼ Distract the cat's attention to a more appropriate activity and cool down his anxiety with a play session.

▼ Use positive reinforcement to show the cat what behaviors are desired.

▼ Make necessary changes to the environment. Provide adequate territory and safety zones for the cats. Block viewing access in the case of redirected aggression; add more litter boxes; separate cats if necessary.

▼ If the problem can't be solved with the help of your veterinarian, seek a consultation with a behaviorist.

▼ If drug therapy is to be used, the cat needs a thorough workup beforehand. Drug therapy must also be combined with behavior modification.

▼ Be realistic about the level of success you may achieve based on case specifics; that is, a cat displaying territorial or status-related aggression may not ever be a lap cat.

keep pieces of treats in your pocket and reward him when he acts appropriately. If he's not food-motivated, use praise, a soothing tone, and petting (if the cat enjoys that).

DRUG THERAPY

Drug therapy can be very helpful in treating feline aggression. It must be used in conjunction with behavior modification, or you merely suppress the behavior, which will likely resurface when the drug is stopped.

Psychoactive drugs aren't "one size fits all." That's why it's important to have an accurate diagnosis of the problem before drugs are prescribed. You must work closely with your veterinarian and behaviorist when deciding to go this route. See chapter 12 for more information.

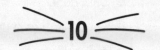

Managing Stress

Stress is a big force in a cat's life. You may not think a cat has much to get stressed over. After all, she doesn't have to go out to work; she doesn't have money problems; and she doesn't have to put her children through college. As you look at your various cats lounging in the sun or playing with their toys, it may be hard to imagine what in their lives could be stressful. Actually, cats are subject to a lot of potential stress. Remember that the cat is a territorial creature of habit, which can put a kitty at risk for lots of stress. Being territorial means it may be stressful when unfamiliar people come to the house. And we all know how stressed out a cat gets when it's time for a visit to the veterinarian. When you're a creature of habit, imagine how confusing it must be to endure a move to a new home or renovation. Look how stressful new cat introductions are. If you read the chapter on understanding the hierarchy, you can appreciate what a delicate balance most multicat environments maintain. Just using the litter box can be risky in a multicat home.

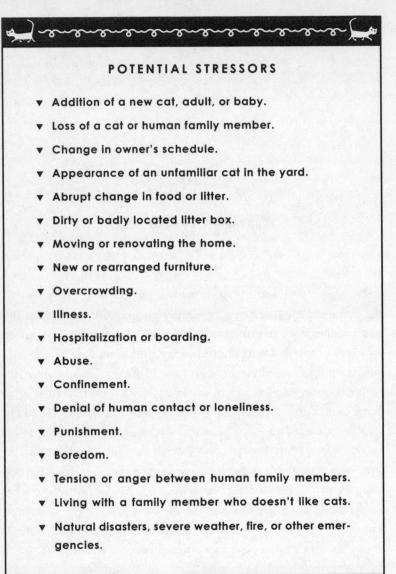

POTENTIAL STRESSORS

▼ Addition of a new cat, adult, or baby.

▼ Loss of a cat or human family member.

▼ Change in owner's schedule.

▼ Appearance of an unfamiliar cat in the yard.

▼ Abrupt change in food or litter.

▼ Dirty or badly located litter box.

▼ Moving or renovating the home.

▼ New or rearranged furniture.

▼ Overcrowding.

▼ Illness.

▼ Hospitalization or boarding.

▼ Abuse.

▼ Confinement.

▼ Denial of human contact or loneliness.

▼ Punishment.

▼ Boredom.

▼ Tension or anger between human family members.

▼ Living with a family member who doesn't like cats.

▼ Natural disasters, severe weather, fire, or other emergencies.

As owners, however well meaning we may be, we often are the cause of stress. We abruptly switch litter or food brands based upon what's on sale; we don't keep the litter box clean enough; we have erratic schedules so our cats never know when we're coming home; we show up one day with a new feline buddy and expect them to be friends right away. We may not notice signs of illness, we use punishment, and we misread what the cats are communicating. We move, we marry, we have children, we divorce, we remarry, we get a dog . . . gosh, it's all so stressful. *Any* change in the environment can stress a cat.

The symptoms of stress can vary greatly, but your best diagnostic tool is your power of observation. Change in any one of your cats is a potential red flag. Watch for changes in appearance, behavior, appetite, and litter box habits. However minor a change may appear, it's worth further investigation.

Stress can have many symptoms. Probably the most common are inappropriate elimination and spray-marking. Cats under stress may also overgroom. Other symptoms include:

Hiding.

Withdrawing from family and companion cats.

Becoming more demanding and constantly seeking attention.

Increased scratching behavior on posts and/or other objects.

Excessive vocalization.

Decrease in appetite.

Aggression directed at a person or a companion cat.

Avoidance of certain locations.

Nongrooming or overgrooming.

Restlessness.

Diarrhea.

Constipation (perhaps because of accumulated hair from over-grooming).

Inappropriate elimination outside of the litter box.

Since the above symptoms are so general and can be connected to a number of medical conditions, you must first have your cat examined by a veterinarian in order to rule out any underlying medical cause. Long-term stress may affect a cat's ability to fight disease. It may also cause recurrences of urinary tract problems in a cat with a history of feline lower urinary tract disease.

In multicat situations, each cat will be affected by and handle stress in different ways. If the majority of your cats adapt easily to change, you may not notice when one or two cats aren't going with the flow. Keep your powers of observation sharp! Look at the relationships between your cats and between the cats and their human family members. Are you inconsistent or inappropriate with your training? Are you frequently gone from home? Have you kept up your part of the litter box responsibilities? When you're home, are you interacting enough with the cats? Have there been *any* changes in your home lately? Have you noticed that one particular cat has withdrawn from the family recently? Perhaps one kitty who normally is very playful now shows a reduced interest in your playtime sessions. Has one cat suddenly become your shadow, meowing constantly? View any change in behavior as an indication that further investigation is needed.

MANAGING STRESS

In a multicat home, overcrowding is a real risk. If you're concerned about the welfare of a stray outdoors, the more responsible and humane thing to do might be to find her a home—just not *your* home. Do you realistically have enough space for multiple cats? If you don't have enough space to create a sanctuary room for a newcomer, it's probably not a good idea to get another cat.

Owners often overlook the need to pick the right cat. A family with six cats may have a wonderfully peaceful home, but another family with only four may be having endless problems if all four are dominant kitties.

When you do decide to bring in another cat, take the time to do a proper introduction. Even if your decision to adopt another cat was impulsive, the introduction process should *never* be. Improper introductions create tremendous stress for all the cats, which will mean stress for you. Provide adequate territory for each cat. Don't skimp on litter boxes, feeding stations, or sleeping areas. Maximize vertical space and create hiding places so all of the cats can find their comfort zones.

Watch for signs of stress and address behavior problems early. Since cats are creatures of habit, it's often obvious when they deviate just the slightest bit from their routines. A potential behavior problem identified and treated early stands a much better chance of successful correction and is far less traumatic for the cat, her companions, and the human family. Stress is a real enemy of cats, and you've probably noticed how stress is an underlying thread throughout almost all the issues discussed in this book. Keep that in mind as you look for the true cause of a particular behavior problem, and work on a plan to correct it. Reducing your cat's stress level should be one of the major components of any behavior modification plan.

It's also very stressful for the cat to get mixed messages about his behavior from different family members. Get all family members on the same page regarding training techniques and how to interact with the cat. Since cats love the familiarity of their routine, be aware of how a potential change will affect them. Take the time to ease them gradually through transitions—whether it's the seemingly minor adjustment of helping them get used to newly installed carpet or the major trauma of losing a loved one. The end of a traumatic event doesn't mean a cat will be able to bounce back emotionally, so watch for signs that your cats are not recovering afterward. In a multicat home it's very easy to miss the fact that a kitty hasn't resumed her normal routine. For example, let's say you move to a new home and do all of the right things to minimize stress for your cats before, during, and immediately after the move. You need to stay alert because one cat may take longer than the others to adjust. Life may be back to normal for the majority of the human and feline family members, but one kitty may still be struggling.

OVERGROOMING

Cats can respond to stress in a number of ways (see list on pages 171–72), but one very common reaction often overlooked by owners is *overgrooming*. Because cats are such fastidious groomers, many times owners assume that the behavior is nothing unusual. Displacement grooming is a normal way for cats to reduce their anxiety and calm themselves during or after a stressful situation, or to release frustration.

You may see this after a cat miscalculates a jump and falls to the floor or if she rolls off a surface while sleeping. The cat will glance around as she grooms. Although it may look as if she's checking to see if anyone noticed her embarrassing moment, it probably has more to do with her need to get her bearings. A cat may also exhibit normal displacement grooming if she wants to jump onto a counter and is repeatedly reprimanded or placed back down on the floor, for example.

Sometimes a cat takes grooming to the extreme. She may groom one spot, or as much of her body as she can reach, to the point of baldness. The skin beneath looks normal, but the hair will just be stubble. This excessive grooming is called psychogenic alopecia.

Before determining that the condition is psychological, a veterinarian must rule out other potential conditions such as parasites, allergies, and hyperthyroidism to name just a few, even if you're sure the cause is behavioral. I'm seeing more and more cats exhibiting overgrooming caused by hyperthyroidism. Hyperesthesia must also be ruled out. If you see bald patches on your cat, don't delay in seeing your veterinarian. One common cause of bald patches is flea allergy dermatitis. Even though you may not actually see a flea because cats are such fastidious groomers, you may see red bumpy skin and hair loss.

If psychogenic alopecia is diagnosed, drug therapy is usually needed to break the behavior pattern. If the cause of the stress is known, it should be removed. If that's not possible, behavior modification must be done to raise the cat's stress tolerance threshold. A consultation with an animal behaviorist may be needed, especially if you can't identify the cause of the stress or it can't be eliminated from your cat's life. With excessive grooming, the behavior may continue even after the stimulus has been removed or decreased, because overgrooming has become a habit by that point. That's where a behavioral treatment plan is necessary.

Hairballs are a side effect of excessive grooming. Keep a close eye on the litter box to see if there's much hair in the feces, and also be aware of how often your cats throw up hairballs. It's often hard to tell who did what in a multicat home, but if you know what's normal for your group of cats, you should be able to spot changes rather quickly. If a cat swallows too much hair, it can cause a blockage in the intestines, which can require surgical removal. The cat may need an oral hairball prevention product on a regular basis while you begin the behavioral treatment plan.

TREATMENT PLAN For excessive grooming, you must first determine the underlying cause. Have your cat examined by a veterinarian to rule out medical possibilities. If it turns out to be behavioral, it's time to put on your detective's hat and figure out what could be causing it.

Use interactive play to help boost confidence and also to redirect some of that displacement anxiety. You can also use the diversion technique described in chapter 5 to redirect the cat and break the pattern. If the cat sits or sprawls out in a certain position before grooming, that's the time to use diversion—*before* he starts to groom. Don't worry if you can't catch those signals, as many cats are secretive groomers. Be aware of body language signals of stress or events that normally stress the cat, and use diversion at that time. The more often you catch the behavior before it actually takes place, the more effective the behavior modification will be.

If your veterinarian determines that drug therapy is needed, he or she may also refer you to an animal behaviorist. With so much attention on psychopharmacology for animal behavior, it can be easy to overlook how important environmental adjustments and behavior modification can be to the overall picture.

Make sure you incorporate those crucial aspects into your treatment plan.

SEPARATION ANXIETY

I wanted to include this topic in this chapter because we often assume that cats can be left alone for long periods of time without any problem. We usually associate separation anxiety with dogs, but cats can actually suffer from it as well, although the symptoms may be different. One of the things many people love about cats is the convenience of being able to leave them for longer than is possible with dogs. Even so, cats do suffer from loneliness and lack of human contact, and abrupt schedule changes can cause problems. Maybe you've gone from working at home to a full-time job outside the home. Suddenly your cats have gone from having you at home most of the day to seeing you for only a few hours at night. This probably is more of an issue in single-cat homes, but it can occur in a multicat situation if any of the cats are especially bonded to you. A cat doesn't have to be in your lap to know you're there. You may not realize at first how much your absence affects the dynamic within the home. Separation anxiety can occur for many reasons: vacations, change in work schedule, or increased absences from change in your social life.

Symptoms of separation anxiety often include litter box problems. A cat may eliminate on your clothes or on your bed because of the strong presence of your scent. She will try to soothe her anxiety by combining her scent with yours, and she may also scratch or chew your belongings. It's important that you not punish a cat for this behavior because it'll just increase her anxiety. Other symptoms can include excessive grooming or excessive vocalization.

TREATMENT PLAN Now more than ever, your cat needs a faith-
fully kept schedule of daily interactive play sessions. You may
even have to increase the number of sessions. Try doing one right
before you leave, then again when you return home, and then
one right before bed. If you can squeeze another in during the
midevening or any other time, that would be great, but try to at
least get two or three in on a daily basis.

Environmental enrichment is also a must for cats with separation anxiety. Make the surroundings more interesting so their
time is occupied when you're not there. A multiperched tree
placed by a window is great for those afternoon naps, climbing,
scratching, and bird-watching sessions. If you can, place a bird
feeder outside the window so the birds can keep your cats enter-
tained. Also, create tunnels out of boxes and bags and hide toys
inside. For food-motivated cats, you can scatter around a few
Play-n-Treat balls.

There are some terrific cat entertainment videos and DVDs
available these days. They showcase birds, mice, fish, and bugs.
My cats come running to the television whenever they hear the
first "tweet" or "chirp" from the sound track. Play the video
when you're home so your cats start learning to find other
sources of entertainment besides being Velcroed to your lap
twenty-four hours a day.

If you have a close neighbor or friend who would be willing to
come over during the day to visit your cats, that would be helpful. Perhaps the friend could conduct a play session or even just
pop one of the cat entertainment videos into the VCR. If the
neighbor could do this for the first week, it may help your cats
get adjusted to your increased absence.

STRANGER ANXIETY

Some of your cats may be social butterflies who charm every person who walks through the door. Other cats may dive under the bed at the sound of the doorbell. Cat-loving visitors who insist that all cats like them often make the situation worse. These are the people who, despite your requests, are determined to reach down to pet the cat or try to hold a kitty who is desperately attempting to get away. It takes only a couple of these episodes for a cat to realize that it's safer just to hide whenever the doorbell rings because whatever is on the other side of the door can't possibly be good.

Cats have their own comfort zones, and some cats can't handle the confusion of strangers "barging" into the territory. Some cats will watch the stranger from a distance. Some may even show aggression if approached, and others just disappear and hide behind the dust bunnies under the furniture. It's very sad to know that the mere act of having a few friends over for dinner will leave one or more of your cats stressed out for the rest of the night.

CATWISE CLUE

Ironically, cats often love the visitors to your home who don't like cats or who are allergic, because the cats know they'll be safe. They can go up to those guests and do a scent investigation and even sit in their laps, and no attempt will be made at holding, petting, or restraining.

TREATMENT PLAN You can help desensitize your cats to visitors with a simple exercise. First, spray Feliway on prominent objects in the living room or wherever you entertain visitors (unless you already have the diffuser plugged in). Next, invite a friend over. This should be a quiet, calm friend whom most of your cats already like. Before entering the house, the friend should spray her shoes and pant cuffs with Feliway. When the guest enters, if the frightened cat is in the area, she should completely ignore her. If the cat chooses to disappear into another room, that's fine. Sit and talk to your friend in a calm voice for a while to give the cat time to settle down. Then, excuse yourself and go to wherever the cat is hiding. You may need to close the door to keep the other cats out for now unless their presence comforts the frightened cat. Allowing her to stay in her hiding place, conduct a very casual, low-key game with an interactive toy. Don't dangle the toy in her face, but rather, just try to get her to focus on the toy's movement. Even if she doesn't come out from hiding, if you can at least ignite some degree of interest, you'll lower her stress level. What's important during this exercise is for your frightened cat to take her cue from you. You're sending the signal that you're not concerned about the "intruder" in the territory and that she shouldn't be either.

After a few minutes of playtime (whether or not your cat actively participates), go back to your company. Leave the door to that room open. If the cat doesn't come out of the room, then wait about fifteen minutes and go back in for another low-key play session and then return to your company again. If the cat does start to venture out, your friend should still ignore her. The cat may choose just to sit at the threshold of the room. If so, that's great progress, because she's starting to feel as if she has some control over the situation. Keep the interactive toy with you and use that to entice the cat if she shows an interest. Don't move the toy toward the company, though. Keep the action within the cat's comfort zone; this is a big step for her. If other cats are around and they start playing with the toy, that's okay, provided it doesn't trigger the frightened cat to slink back out of the room. You have to play this by ear based on the relationships between the cats in your home.

After several visits, you should be able to hand the interactive toy to your friend so she can engage in a play session with the cat. Also, you can then start inviting a different friend over so your cats get used to various people.

LESS STRESSFUL VISITS TO THE VETERINARIAN

I couldn't write a chapter on stress without covering this topic. Even though you try to eliminate as much stress from the lives of your cats as possible, they do have to see the veterinarian. Veterinarians do so much good for our animals, it's a shame that pets view the person in the white coat as the enemy. There are some ways to make these visits a bit less stressful. Although the veterinary clinic may never be a place a cat looks forward to visiting, at least we can make it a bit more bearable.

TREATMENT PLAN If you have a kitten, the time to start getting her used to the veterinarian's office is right now. It's also good to get her used to being in her carrier and traveling in the car. Take her to the veterinarian's office just for social visits—the earlier a cat gets used to carriers, car travel, and being handled and petted by the veterinary staff, the better. Even if you have a new adult cat in your home and you don't know how she reacts to travel and being at the veterinary clinic, you should start building her

tolerance. It may have to be a bit more gradual, but having a cat
who is comfortable in a carrier and at the veterinary clinic will
pay you in spades if you are ever faced with an emergency.

No matter how calm your cat has been during previous visits
to the veterinarian, you must transport her in a carrier. First of
all, it's dangerous to drive with a cat loose in the car because she
can easily get wedged under the accelerator or brake pedal. She
can also cause a dangerous distraction. In an accident, the cat
stands a much better chance of survival if confined in a carrier. In
fact, you should strap the carrier in with the seat belt. You can
put the belt around the whole carrier or loop the belt through the
handle. Another important reason for the carrier is that you
never know if this visit will cause your cat's stress-o-meter to go
over the top. It might be because of another animal in the waiting
room or maybe a painful procedure. Don't risk it—always use a
carrier. If you have a cat who gets terrified or actually gets fractious, you may want to use the type of carrier where the top and
bottom unscrew and come apart. Sometimes being able to remain
in the bottom half of the familiar carrier will reduce a cat's anxiety.

Unless it's an emergency, schedule your veterinary appointments for the least busy time of the day. If your veterinarian
tends to get behind schedule, make your appointment for early in
the morning. That's also a good time if your cats react negatively
to other animal scents, because the clinic will have been cleaned
the night before or maybe first thing in the morning and the
scents of the various clients will have been removed from the
waiting room.

Spray the inside corners of the carrier with Feliway twenty
minutes before putting the cat inside. Each cat should go in her
own carrier so you don't have the risk of aggressive behavior
caused by heightened stress.

If you're taking more than one cat at a time, try to match up the cats who get along best, if possible. Even though the cats will all be in carriers, being in a confined and moving environment such as a car may elevate their stress levels. If one cat is exceptionally vocal when under stress, keep in mind that she may excite the other cats in the car.

Bring a light towel or shirt to drape over the carrier if your cat gets excited in the car or while in the waiting room. If your cat is fine in the car but freaks out once you step into the clinic, wait in your car until it's your turn and ask the receptionist to either signal you at the door or call your cell phone.

Feliway can be used on the examination table before you bring your cat inside.

You may have a "window of opportunity" with a particular cat. Some cats tend to be very fearful at first but then settle down after being in the clinic for a while. With another cat you may have to move quickly because she's okay for the first ten minutes and then *bam,* in the eleventh minute she turns into all teeth and claws. Know your windows of opportunity with each cat so you can coordinate the veterinary exam accordingly.

If any of your cats have to be hospitalized, bring a couple of paper bags and a couple of T-shirts that contain your scent. The cat will feel more secure if she has a place to hide, so ask the staff to cuff the paper bag, place it on its side, and line the bottom with the T-shirt. If the bag is too large for the cage, you can roll the cuff over a number of times until it fits.

I always bring some litter, too, so my cat doesn't have to deal with an abrupt change. Depending on what is being done and whether the cat will be eating while hospitalized, I also bring some food. The more familiar associations there are to comfort your kitty, the better.

Sometimes a cat who has stayed home may exhibit aggressive behavior when another cat returns from the veterinary clinic. Set up a temporary sanctuary room so the returning cat can have a calm place to relax and take on the scents of the home again before reacquainting herself with the others. Whether it's the returning cat who gets agitated or the cats who stayed home who react negatively, this is the best way to address the situation.

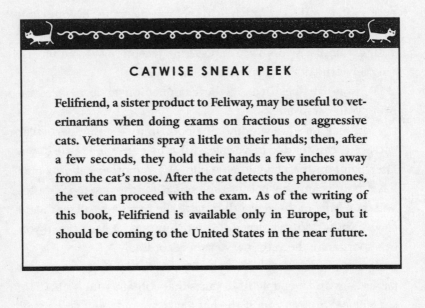

CATWISE SNEAK PEEK

Felifriend, a sister product to Feliway, may be useful to veterinarians when doing exams on fractious or aggressive cats. Veterinarians spray a little on their hands; then, after a few seconds, they hold their hands a few inches away from the cat's nose. After the cat detects the pheromones, the vet can proceed with the exam. As of the writing of this book, Felifriend is available only in Europe, but it should be coming to the United States in the near future.

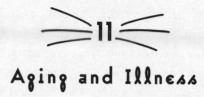

Aging and Illness

Life in your multicat household may go along smoothly for years and then a sudden illness can cause a drastic change within the hierarchy of relationships. It may affect the dynamic between a couple of cats or it may affect everyone. When one cat gets sick, it's not just a crisis for that individual cat—it's a crisis for everyone in the home. Being prepared will help you handle the emotional aspects of illness as well as the physical. This also applies to aging cats, but with aging, the changes in relationships may be missed because they creep up subtly as the cats get older. You may not notice a distinct change until one kitty is no longer able to jump and climb or perhaps becomes grouchy when disturbed while lounging in the sun. The sooner you start preparing for those potential changes, the easier the golden years will be for your elderkitties.

THE ILL CAT

Obviously, a cat with a potentially contagious illness should be separated from the rest of the cat community, but a cat with a chronic illness that isn't contagious can still be an active member of the feline family with some modifications to the environment. Cats with chronic problems may not do well within the group and may need to be separated if the pain or discomfort makes them less tolerant, aggressive, or fearful. The cat may continue to get along with one or two of his companions, depending on personalities and past relationships, so you may find that the companion cats can move between the sick cat's sanctuary and the main part of the house as well. The main thing you don't want to do with an ill cat is increase his stress. Make sure his surroundings are secure and comfortable—whether that includes all of his companions, some of them, or none of them.

Environmental modifications can do wonders for a cat suffering from a long-term illness. The following sections refer to aging cats, but all the basic techniques will apply to ill cats as well.

THE ELDERKITTY IN THE FAMILY

If you have older cats in your household, you want to do all you can to make sure their senior years are comfortable and happy. That can take some careful planning in a household filled with cats of various ages.

As a cat ages, his senses may start to decline. If an older cat has decreased hearing, come slowly into his field of vision before petting him or picking him up. With decreased vision, create safe access to his favorite places. Don't rearrange furniture and don't relocate food bowls or litter boxes. His ease in getting around depends on familiarity with pathways. Watch how a cat's deteriorating senses may affect his relationship with other cats. Make sure he doesn't get startled by revved-up young members of your feline or human family.

Cats who are ill or older ones with decreased senses or mobility may lose status in the hierarchy. Cats are survival-oriented, and it's normal for stronger, healthier kitties to assume the higher status in the group. Even though this is a normal aspect of cat life, you want to ensure your older or ill cats don't get picked on or pushed out of their favorite areas. Watch the dynamics of the group and use the playtime diversion technique to distract a potentially aggressive cat. Prevent territorial takeovers so your older or ill kitty won't have to worry when he wants to rest his tired bones on a sunny window perch.

VETERINARY EXAMS

Now more than ever, an aging cat needs to be seen by the veterinarian on a regular basis. Age-related problems such as CRF (chronic renal failure), diabetes, and arthritis, to name just a few, are relatively common, but early diagnosis will enable you and your veterinarian to establish a medical plan and help your cat stay healthy and comfortable for many more years. Even though an old cat may naturally slow down and sleep more, some age-related problems aren't immediately obvious. Keeping an eye on his physical state, monitoring his food and water intake and litter box habits, and scheduling regular veterinary checkups are valuable in ensuring good health for your beloved old friend. Accurate diagnosis of underlying medical problems can also explain an elderkitty's behavior changes that could be affecting everyone in the household. With an older cat who will be making more visits to the veterinarian, keep in mind that this may cause him stress as well as the other cats.

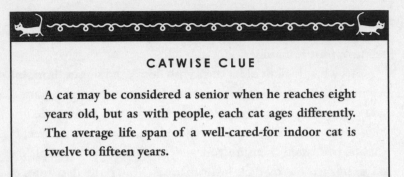

CATWISE CLUE

A cat may be considered a senior when he reaches eight years old, but as with people, each cat ages differently. The average life span of a well-cared-for indoor cat is twelve to fifteen years.

FEEDING Your veterinarian may put your older cat on a senior formula food, or on a special diet if he has a medical condition. This can be tough in a multicat home if the cat wants to eat what everyone else is eating. Then there are also, believe it or not, the households where the *other* cats want the senior cat's prescription food instead of their own.

To ensure that your older cat gets the appropriate food, you may have to schedule his feeding so you can monitor his intake. If the older cat doesn't jump onto elevated areas anymore, you can keep his food on ground level and put the other cats' food on a higher surface. That will work only if the prescription diet isn't appealing to the other cats. Otherwise, scheduled feeding, as described in chapter 6, of several small meals per day will be your best bet.

If you do decide on scheduled meals, don't offer just one or two meals a day, because an older cat doesn't have the top-notch digestive system he had in his youth. Cats in general do better with multiple small meals. If the senior cat is getting nosed out of the food or you're concerned that he's not getting his share, you may even have to feed him separately in addition to monitoring his meals.

ENVIRONMENTAL MODIFICATIONS

In his prime, your older cat may have been able to leap from the floor to the top of dresser in one graceful move. Now, however, he may hardly be able to jump up into a favorite chair. Since cats love elevated places, regardless of their age, you may have to make some adjustments to accommodate him.

Cat trees are great because they allow cats to gradually climb to the top perches. For some older cats, the perches may be too far apart, so look for a tree with numerous closely spaced perches, or add a perch or two to an existing tree. The perches on the tree should be wide for ease when ascending or descending and U-shaped for maximum comfort. You might even want to lay folded towels on the perches for added warmth and softness.

A heated window perch is great for a senior cat. If he has trouble reaching it, create a ramp or place furniture in front to provide him easy access. If an older cat likes lower hiding places, get him a fleece-lined A-frame bed or a heated bed. Having them in different rooms is a great way to help him maintain his territory and continue to enjoy the parts of the house he likes. If he has always enjoyed sleeping on the bed and can no longer make that jump, construct or purchase a pet ramp. You can buy commercial pet ramps through mail-order companies (check the ad section in the back of your favorite cat-related magazine), or build a small set of stairs yourself. The stairway should have two or three steps, depending upon the height of your bed, and the steps should be wide and carpeted. If you're not a do-it-yourselfer, you can have it built for you. We built a little stairway for Albie, my twenty-year-old cat, so he could easily get to his favorite sunny window perch.

THE LITTER BOX

An older cat, especially one with arthritis, may have difficulty climbing in and out of the litter box. A low-sided box or two will make it more comfortable for him.

Monitor the cat's litter box habits so you'll be alerted to any potential underlying medical problem. I know this can be a trick in a multicat home, but since cats are territorial creatures of habit, you may notice that certain cats tend to frequent specific boxes. Be understanding of litter box mishaps with an aging cat. Decreased bladder control may make it more difficult for him to get to the box in time. A cat with diabetes or chronic renal failure (CRF) may also have accidents. You might find that a cat has uri-nated in his sleep as well. Because of deteriorating senses, a cat may sleep more soundly and not be aware of the cues from his bladder until it's too late. Be very tolerant of this, but do make sure you clean urine off your cat immediately to prevent scalding of the skin, to reduce his stress from having to do so much self-grooming, and to prevent companion cats from having a negative reaction to him. You may need to increase the number of litter boxes now so an older cat won't have as far to walk to reach one.

The scent of an ill cat can create anxiety in some companion cats. A companion may be upset by the strange odor of a med-icated or ill cat's urine, so he may start eliminating outside of the box. Scoop litter boxes meticulously. Watch for signs of trouble, and increase the number of boxes so the concerned cat has more options. If a companion starts showing fear or aggression toward an ill cat, you may have to separate them to avoid stressing your sick kitty.

PLAYTIME AND EXERCISE An older cat may no longer be able to do those acrobatic leaps that he was once famous for or pounce on a toy with lightning speed, but he'll still enjoy play-time. In fact, encouraging your older cat to remain active will be an important part of maintaining his health. For a sluggish diges-tive system, exercise will help improve intestinal motility and also improve circulation. From an emotional standpoint, maintaining a playtime schedule may also keep that spark going so an aging kitty doesn't become too sedentary or depressed.

The playtime routine will have to be modified to fit an older cat's medical and physical condition. Don't force a cat to do things he no longer can comfortably do such as jumping, run-ning, or climbing. Keep the movements of the toy within the cat's ability, even if that means just wiggling it on the floor a few inches in front of him. Play sessions may have to be shorter as well. If you match the game to the individual cat's ability, he'll enjoy it much more and will benefit from the exercise, even if it just involves pawing at the toy. Any amount of activity will bene-fit a cat in his senior years. Be sensitive to his ability and desire. Don't overdo.

Because an older cat may not have the ability to engage in a group interactive play session with the youngsters in your home, you may need to set aside time for special one-on-one sessions with him. If you have a couple of older cats who are good friends and will play cooperatively, you can do a mini group session with just them. Otherwise, do individual sessions so you can focus on a senior cat's specific needs.

Even if you have an older kitty who acts like a youngster and effortlessly leaps from chair to cat tree, be sensitive to his move-ments during playtime. Don't stress his joints by encouraging high leaps or have him racing to exhaustion after a toy. Remem-ber, much of a cat's hunting technique involves the mental stim-ulation of stalking and planning. Older cats need that mental stimulation as much as the physical activity.

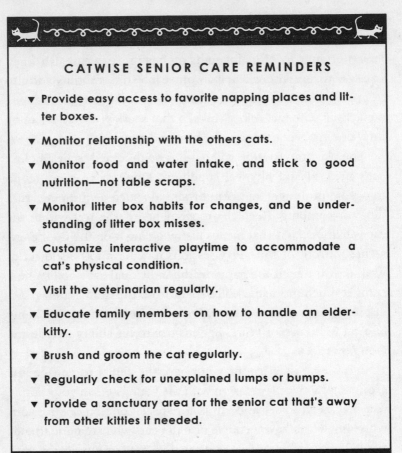

CATWISE SENIOR CARE REMINDERS

▼ Provide easy access to favorite napping places and litter boxes.

▼ Monitor relationship with the others cats.

▼ Monitor food and water intake, and stick to good nutrition—not table scraps.

▼ Monitor litter box habits for changes, and be understanding of litter box misses.

▼ Customize interactive playtime to accommodate a cat's physical condition.

▼ Visit the veterinarian regularly.

▼ Educate family members on how to handle an elderkitty.

▼ Brush and groom the cat regularly.

▼ Regularly check for unexplained lumps or bumps.

▼ Provide a sanctuary area for the senior cat that's away from other kitties if needed.

NAP TIME An older cat loves his naps now more than ever. Make sure your elderkitty has easy access to his favorite spots and can nap undisturbed. If you have feline youngsters in the home who view a napping senior as the perfect target for practicing their pouncing skills, then some periodic separation is needed.

THE ULTIMATE SADNESS: DEATH AND MOURNING

The loss of a family member, whether human or feline, is always devastating. It turns our lives upside down, and it takes all of our strength to find our way back to being able to go on with "normal" life. Your cats feel that pain as well and grieve the loss of family members. Animals have the added confusion of not understanding why *you're* not acting the way you normally do.

If any of your cats are older, then although this may not be a subject you want to think about, it's something that's inevitable. It's also something that will greatly affect the other cats in the home, so it's better to be prepared for how to help everyone through this.

You may not have considered that cats grieve, but they do. Look at it from their point of view. They suddenly lose a companion (or human family member) and don't understand where that person or animal has gone. Then they start to notice that their whole world has changed. Their owner is acting very strangely, and the dynamics of the kitty hierarchy have changed as well. Even worse, they might find themselves alone.

In your effort to provide comfort to your grieving cats, you may hold or cuddle them more. Be careful about how much you do and the way you do it. Keep in mind that cats are emotional sponges and are highly sensitive to the emotions you convey. You don't want to set off the alarm bells in your cats' heads that this is truly the end of their world. Balance your cuddling and holding with interactive playtime and casual, normal tone-of-voice conversations. When you do cuddle your cats, try to do it in the same way you used to so it's not too intense. Even though playtime may be the last thing you want to do right now, your cats need the security of their routine. They need to know that although something devastating has happened, most of their world remains the same. That's why, as hard as it may be, you need to keep your tone and demeanor as light and normal as possible.

Something happens in a multicat home when one of the cats passes away—the hierarchy may go through some shifting, with some renegotiations of territory. You're probably well aware of how *adding* a cat affects the hierarchy and causes territorial jockeying, but it also occurs when a cat is taken away from the environment. The entire cat household may go through hierarchical shifts. The severity of it will depend on the status and personality of the cat who passed away. The cats will probably go through a grieving period, during which they'll search for their friend and stay close to his favorite spots. They may vocalize more, and some may stop eating. A few may seek out your attention more. Some cats deal with the anxiety by overgrooming, and others may totally withdraw from the rest of the family. Watch your cats' reactions during this period so you can catch potential problems before they become ongoing. In addition to interactive playtime, increase the entertainment factor in your home with cat entertainment videos, catnip parties, and so forth. If a cat appears to be really struggling with the grief or if he stops eating, consult your veterinarian.

When a kitty passes away, wait until everyone (feline and human) has finished grieving before adding another cat. The newcomer shouldn't have to endure unfair expectations and comparisons or be seen as a "replacement."

Although you can't predict how particular cats may react to the death of a companion or family member, just do your best to stay alert and provide what they need. They'll return the favor by being there with the purrs and cat kisses you need to get yourself through this difficult time.

Extra Help

If you find yourself trying to solve a behavior problem without success, take a deep breath and relax because there's help out there. Don't feel as if you've failed, because behavior problems can be very complex. Because cats can't tell us what's bothering them in a language we understand, we have to use our best detective skills. It's very hard for some owners to separate themselves from the emotion of the situation enough to be objective. Some problems are simply too dangerous to try to handle on your own, as in cases of certain aggressive behaviors.

Before trying to correct a behavior problem, it's very important to understand "normal" behavior. For example, your cat may be growling and showing signs of aggression, but if it's directed at an unfamiliar cat, then it's very normal. Once you know what's normal, you can apply appropriate behavior modification. If you aren't sure what is or isn't normal, that's another reason to get professional advice.

GETTING PROFESSIONAL HELP

Behavior counseling has become an increasingly popular field, and there are now more options available to owners than ever before. When it comes to seeking professional help, your first step should always be to talk with your veterinarian. Many veterinarians are informed about animal behavior and are better able to diagnose and treat certain problems.

Because cats can't tell us what's wrong, any kind of diagnosis must first rule out underlying medical causes, and then must take into account medical history, behavior, environmental circumstances, other cats/pet/people in the home, and the context in which the behavior is displayed. Your veterinarian will need all of this extremely valuable information, and you are his/her eyes and ears for everything that occurs outside of his/her office.

ANIMAL BEHAVIORISTS

After your veterinarian is familiar with the behavior problem and ruled out underlying medical causes, he or she may refer you to an animal behaviorist. If your veterinarian doesn't know of a behaviorist in your area, there's information in the Appendix of this book on how to find one.

Some animal behaviorists, are certified and others aren't. Anyone can call him- or herself a behaviorist, but it doesn't mean they have the appropriate knowledge. The safest route is to contact a certified applied animal behaviorist. If you decide not to use a certified behaviorist, then choose a behaviorist with an excellent reputation who comes recommended by a veterinarian. There are many excellent noncertified behaviorists, but you don't want to trust your cats to just anyone. Even though I'm not certified myself, I have worked in this field for many, many years, and I've seen too many unqualified people give incorrect advice. For more specific information on certification, see the Appendix.

A behaviorist is a true "pet detective." The information you supply will be the crucial clues he or she needs to piece together a diagnosis and treatment plan. Some behaviorists (like me) work on a house call basis, and some do clinic appointments. If there isn't a behaviorist in your area, you can find one who does phone or e-mail consultations. This is obviously not as ideal as having a behaviorist see the cat in person, but if there's no way you can travel for a clinic appointment, it's better than nothing. For me, I need to see the cats and their environments, so I only do house calls.

Behaviorists who do clinic appointments will also schedule all necessary diagnostic workups for your cat. Behaviorists who work on a house call basis will work with your veterinarian or an animal hospital if tests need to be performed. The behaviorist will require an in-depth behavioral history on your cat. He or she will ask you many questions, and you may be asked to fill out a client questionnaire before the consultation.

Once a diagnosis is made, the behaviorist will map out the treatment plan. Keep in mind that behavior modification takes time. A problem that has been ongoing for quite some time won't be corrected in one afternoon. After the diagnosis, the success of a behavioral treatment plan is totally dependent upon how well the owner sticks to the plan.

PHARMACOLOGICAL INTERVENTION There are times when behavior modification alone can't change a behavior problem. Drug therapy, however, isn't an answer by itself or an easy fix. It can only be successful when used along with behavior modification. If you don't change the kitty's responses or associations, he will have to stay on the medication forever, and if you take the cat off the drug, the undesirable behavior may resurface. Psychoactive drugs, if used inappropriately, only treat the symptoms and may end up masking the real problem. Psychoactive drugs are not "one size fits all" and must only be prescribed by a veterinarian or veterinary behaviorist. *Do not* medicate a cat on your own using any psychoactive drug you may take yourself. Also, don't give a drug to a cat that was prescribed for another cat. Many drugs have potentially serious side effects, and cats have very sensitive systems. Extreme caution must be used when deciding to put a cat on drug therapy.

The use of psychoactive drugs on cats is considered "extralabel." This refers to drugs used in veterinary medicine that were intended for humans and are not FDA-approved for use in animals. It also refers to a drug approved for one animal species that is then used in another species, as well as drugs used for specific medical conditions for which they weren't FDA-approved. Extralabel applies to more than just behavioral medications, and although many of these drugs have been widely prescribed and successfully used for years, they can still be risky. Veterinary extralabel use is allowed and, in most cases, provides animals with the benefits of many excellent drugs, but you still need to be educated about *any* drug prescribed for your pet.

BEFORE DRUG THERAPY IS PRESCRIBED:

* The veterinarian must do a thorough medical examination, including all appropriate diagnostic testing. Cats should have a blood profile, including a complete blood count (CBC). An electrocardiogram is also recommended, especially for older cats and those with a history of medical problems.

* An in-depth behavioral history on the cat is needed. Your veterinarian must know the behavioral history because a drug may have an undesirable behavioral side effect.

* Always try behavior modification first and give it time to work.

* The veterinarian may refer you to a behaviorist.

If the veterinarian or behaviorist prescribes a drug for your cat and you're concerned about your ability to administer it, find out if it can be compounded into a more palatable form. A compounding pharmacist can create a flavored liquid or paste for many veterinary prescriptions. If there isn't a compounding pharmacy in your area, check the Internet because a prescription can be called in by your veterinarian and then shipped directly to you. In the case of some drugs, the actual prescription will need to be mailed in by the veterinarian. In addition to flavored medications, some prescriptions can be reformulated into a transdermal delivery system. With the transdermal, you apply a cream to the inside tip of the ear where it absorbs into the bloodstream.

THE RESPONSIBILITY OF THE FAMILY DURING TREATMENT

When starting a behavioral treatment plan, all members of the family must be willing to cooperate. Although one or two adults will be primarily responsible for the specifics of the problem, it's important that everyone remain consistent so the cat doesn't get mixed messages.

It's also important for everyone in the family to understand why the problem occurred in the first place and how to prevent

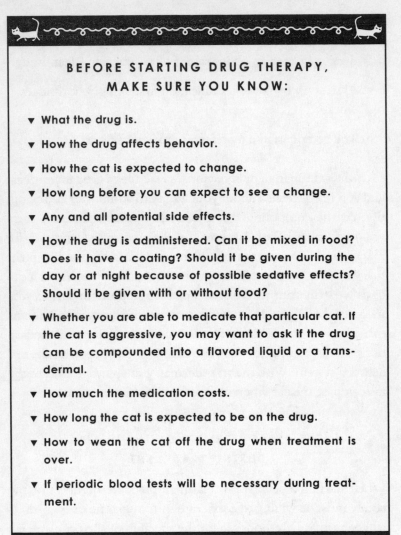

BEFORE STARTING DRUG THERAPY, MAKE SURE YOU KNOW:

▼ What the drug is.

▼ How the drug affects behavior.

▼ How the cat is expected to change.

▼ How long before you can expect to see a change.

▼ Any and all potential side effects.

▼ How the drug is administered. Can it be mixed in food? Does it have a coating? Should it be given during the day or at night because of possible sedative effects? Should it be given with or without food?

▼ Whether you are able to medicate that particular cat. If the cat is aggressive, you may want to ask if the drug can be compounded into a flavored liquid or a trans-dermal.

▼ How much the medication costs.

▼ How long the cat is expected to be on the drug.

▼ How to wean the cat off the drug when treatment is over.

▼ If periodic blood tests will be necessary during treatment.

future problems. Education is your best tool, so take the time to teach everyone old enough to understand what the cats need and how they communicate. This is the time when you can also make sure family members don't misinterpret the motivation behind a cat's behavior. For example, a family member may feel the cat misbehaves because *"she hates me"* or *"she's getting back at me."* Warn family members about losing their tempers. Even though this may be a time of crisis for everyone, if someone loses his or her temper, the cat's stress level will skyrocket. Family dynamics will influence the success of the treatment plan. Spouses or family members who yell at each other can keep the home in a constant state of stress. This can keep all of the cats in highly reactive states as well. The family needs to stay committed to the treatment plan. Problems aren't corrected overnight. Everyone should be prepared for behavior modification to take time.

REHOMING AND EUTHANASIA

It's not something anyone wants to think about, but some owners do suddenly find themselves feeling as if they've reached the end of their rope. Before you decide to place a cat in another home or euthanize one for behavior problems, please seek the advice of your veterinarian and a behaviorist as well. Too many animals are relinquished to shelters or put to death for behavior problems that could have been corrected.

If safety is the issue and you're worried that one of your cats may hurt a family member, keep the cat in a separate area of the home and seek your veterinarian's advice immediately.

Sometimes a cat may do better in another environment. The behavior might be triggered by stimulus in your home that can't be removed. In that case, the cat may be happier in an environment without that stimulus.

If you do rehome a cat because of a behavior problem, you have a moral obligation to disclose that information. The cat may do beautifully in the new home, but the prospective owners have a right to know the history. It will also be crucial for them to have this information in order to do appropriate behavior modification.

Sadly, euthanasia is all too often a quick fix for some owners with so-called "problem" cats who urinate, scratch, or cry when and where it's inconvenient for their owners. How tragic to end a healthy cat's life for a behavior problem that may be treatable. If you're at the point where you're considering euthanizing a cat, please seek your veterinarian's counsel immediately and that of a behavioral specialist. If you can't afford an in-home or clinic visit, please contact a behaviorist who does phone or e-mail consultations. If euthanasia does ultimately end up being the recommendation, you may feel much less guilty if you know you exhausted all other avenues first. The behavior modification process may also help you avoid problems with another animal in the future.

APPENDIX

To locate a behaviorist nearest your area, you can contact the **Animal Behavior Society** at www.animalbehavior.org. Behaviorists are listed in the "Directory" section.

You can also go to the **American Veterinary Society of Animal Behaviorists** at www.avma.org/avsab.

Many veterinary universities do client appointments in their behavioral departments as well. Referrals can be made through your veterinarian. Check the veterinary university closest to you.

VETERINARY ORGANIZATIONS

American Veterinary Medical Association
Suite 100
1931 Meacham Road
Schaumburg, IL 60173
847-925-8070
www.avma.org

There's a section on the Web site for pet owners.

American Holistic Veterinary Medical Association
2218 Old Emmorton Road
Bel Air, MD 21015
410-569-0795
www.ahvma.org

American Board of Veterinary Practitioners
Suite 220
618 Church Street
Nashville, TN 37219
615-254-3687
www.abvp.com

American Board of Feline Practitioners
Suite 220
618 Church Street
Nashville, TN 37219
615-259-7788
800-204-3514
www.aafponline.org

American Animal Hospital Association
P.O. Box 150899
Denver, CO 80215
www.aahanet.org *(for veterinary professionals)*
www.healthypet.com *(for pet owners)*

ANIMAL WELFARE AND PET OWNER EDUCATION

ASPCA
424 East 92nd Street
New York, NY 10128
212-876-7700
www.aspca.org

Behavior counseling is available through the ASPCA.

American Humane Association
63 Inverness Drive East
Englewood, CO 80112
866-242-1877
www.americanhumane.org

Site has valuable information for pet owners.

Humane Society of the United States
2100 L Street, N.W.
Washington, DC 20037
www.hsus.org

Tree House Animal Foundation
1212 West Carmen Avenue
Chicago, IL 60640
773-784-5488
www.treehouseanimals.org

Delta Society
Suite 101
580 Naches Avenue, S.W.
Renton, WA 98055
425-226-7357
www.deltasociety.org

PRODUCT MANUFACTURERS

TopCat Products
615-874-1221
www.topcatproducts.com

Scratching posts and scratching pads.

Go-Cat
3248 Mulliken Road
Charlotte, MI 48813
517-543-7519

Da Bird, cat entertainment videos, and DVDs.

Dragonfly Cat Toys
P.O. Box 22
Deerton, MI 49822-0022
www.dragonflycattoys.com
e-mail: doctomreed@yahoo.com

Dragonfly cat toy.

Cats with an Attitude, Inc.
P.O. Box 88019
Phoenix, AZ 85080-8019
623-580-8573

Swizzle Teaser.

Cat Dancer Products
5145 Green Valley Road
Neenah, WI 54956
www.catdancer.com

Cat Dancer and Cat Charmer.

Angelical Cat Company
Unit 206
102 Commerce Center
5405 Northwest 102nd Avenue
Sunrise, FL 33351
954-747-3629
www.angelicalcat.com

Cat trees.

Farnam Pet Products
Phoenix, AZ 85013
800-234-2269
www.farnampet.com

Feliway spray and Feliway Comfort Zone diffuser.

Fe-Lines, Inc.
888-697-2873
www.stickypaws.com

Sticky Paws.

Cosmic Catnip Company
133 South Burhams Boulevard
Hagerstown, MD 21740
888-226-7642
www.cosmicpet.com

Cosmic Catnip Alpine Scratcher as well as other horizontal scratching pads.

Tots in Mind
290 Broadway
Methuen, MA 01844
800-626-0339
www.totsinmind.com

Cozy Crib Tent.

Our Pet's Company
1300 East Street
Fairport Harbor, OH 44077
440-354-6500
www.ourpets.com

Play-n-Treat, Play-n-Squeak.

Pets 'n People, Inc.
Suite 400
1815 Via El Prado
Redondo Beach, CA 90277
310-540-3727

Nature's Miracle Stain & Odor Remover, Nature's Miracle Urine Odor Source Locator (black light).

ADDITIONAL READING

Johnson-Bennett, Pam. *Think Like a Cat: How to Raise a Well-Adjusted Cat—Not a Sour Puss.* New York: Penguin USA, 2000.

Johnson-Bennett, Pam. *Hiss and Tell: True Stories from the Files of a Cat Shrink.* New York: Penguin USA, 2001.

INDEX